TABLE OF CONTENTS

MW00343890

INTRODUCTION

In the mid-1980s, a group of seventeen teachers in Oregon formed the Analytical Writing Assessment Committee. Their goal was to create a logical rubric to help teachers evaluate their students' writing in a consistent and fair way. They identified six key elements that should appear in every piece of student writing and developed scoring guides for each one. The result was the six traits rubrics.

What Are the Six Traits and the Six Traits Rubrics?

The six traits are elements of writing that most students already know and use. Specifically, they are **1) ideas and content, 2) organization, 3) voice, 4) word choice, 5) sentence fluency,** and **6) conventions.** The rubrics provide a consistent vocabulary and a clear set of criteria for evaluating each trait on a scale of 5–3–1. The rubrics identify the benchmarks of excellent, adequate, and poor writing for each trait. Teachers, parents, and students may use the rubrics to get an overview of how well a paper articulates ideas and expresses a point of view, voice, and style.

How Do the Six Traits Help Teachers and Parents Evaluate Students' Work?

The six traits rubrics help teachers and parents focus when they read and evaluate a student's paper. By providing a consistent vocabulary for discussing and thinking about writing and by offering a standard set of criteria, the rubrics help teachers evaluate a paper quickly, fairly, and accurately. The ideas contained in the rubrics are concepts that students have already learned. The rubrics help the teacher evaluate how a particular student is writing at a particular point in time, for a particular writing assignment.

How Do the Six Traits Help Students?

The six traits put students in control of their own writing. The rubrics offer them a clear language and a logical set of criteria for evaluating different aspects of their work. The rubrics break down the process of self-evaluation into six steps. By focusing on one trait at a time, students can get a sense of the strengths and weaknesses of their writing. In other words, the rubrics provide a balanced overview of how the student has used the six key elements in the writing. For example, after writing a draft of a persuasive essay, a student can use the six traits rubrics to discover that her ideas and organization are strong but that her voice and word choice are a little weak, her sentences tend to run on, and she really needs to review the rules for using commas. She can use the specific criteria in the rubrics to pinpoint the areas that need "polish."

In addition, students can use the six traits rubrics to evaluate the writing of their peers in order to help other students with their revising process and development as writers. A student evaluator can reach an authentic assessment of where the writer stands with that piece of writing at that point in his or her development as a writer and can offer helpful feedback to the writer.

How Do the Six Traits Rubrics "Fit" with the Writing Process?

Student writers can integrate the rubrics at each step in the writing process—not just when they revise their work. For example, in the prewriting stage, writers focus on ideas and content and begin thinking about organizational strategies. In the writing stage, they focus more on content, organization, and voice. As they revise and edit their drafts, they make sure that their ideas and organizational strategies are sound, their voice and word choice are appropriate, and their sentences add structure, rhythm, and style to their writing. As they proofread, they concentrate on their sentence structures and their implementation of writing conventions. Good writers already synthesize ideas, organization, voice, word choice, sentence structure, and conventions as they prepare their papers. The six traits rubrics help students at every level examine these elements and see how they integrate in their writing.

How to Use this Book

PART ONE of this book provides an overview and explanation of the six traits. Each trait is described, and background information and terms are provided to help students understand how the trait is used in both writing and evaluating. In addition, Part One provides an overview of the writing process and an explanation of how to integrate the six traits into each stage. The section includes an at-a-glance chart to show how the six traits are used at various stages of the writing process.

PART TWO contains student-written essays (expository, persuasive, and narrative) and evaluations of those essays based on the six traits rubrics. The objective is to show students how they can use the six traits to evaluate another person's writing. In addition, Part Two contains three student essays that students can evaluate on their own. They can practice applying the rubrics to another person's writing.

PART THREE shows students how to use the six traits at each stage of the writing process. First it provides a review of how to read and analyze a writing prompt. This review is followed by three writing workshops (expository, persuasive, and narrative). The writing workshops guide students through the process of writing while considering the six traits. In addition, each writing workshop is followed by six writing prompts geared toward that same mode of writing. The prompts are similar to those found on many state-mandated tests, and they challenge students to write in a particular mode at varying levels of difficulty.

PART FOUR contains nearly two dozen trait-specific worksheets to help students at each stage of the writing process. Students can use the worksheets to help develop specific writing projects, to improve their mastery of a particular trait, or to practice skills for revising and editing their work.

PART FIVE contains support materials that will help students use the rubrics and refine their own writing skills. It includes the six traits rubrics for both teacher evaluators and student or self-evaluators. There is also a blank evaluation form that students can use for evaluating their own or another student's writing. Finally, Part Five includes an answer key for the practice essays as well as the worksheets.

PART ONE

Overview of the Six Traits and the Writing Process

IDEAS AND CONTENT

Ideas and content are the most important parts of any paper. They are the paper's message—its theme, main idea, or story line. A paper without ideas is like a house built on swampy land. Without firm ground to support it, it will wobble and fall. A paper with a firm foundation of good ideas will, like a soaring skyscraper or majestic castle, make people pay attention and show them something interesting.

Before you try to determine if a paper has good ideas and content, you may want to review the following terms: **main idea, details, purpose,** and **audience**. These elements contribute to ideas and content.

Main Idea

A **main idea** is the most important point in a piece of writing. It may be stated directly, but sometimes a writer will hint at the main idea by dropping clues. That is an implied main idea. Whether it is directly stated or just implied, the main idea should be clear, and the rest of the paper should be built around it. All the other ideas should relate in some way to the main idea.

Details

Details are the supporting ideas that help a writer flesh out an idea. Details for a persuasive paper might take the form of evidence—facts, statistics, examples, and anecdotes—that helps the writer convince readers to think or do something. In a narrative or expository paper, details help readers imagine a new idea or a particular event.

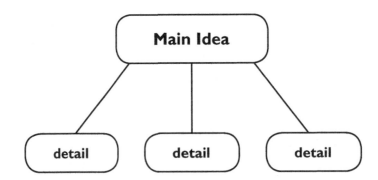

Purpose

The **writer's purpose** is the reason he or she is writing. The writer may want to share information, express feelings, or influence the way others think or act. Keeping the purpose in mind helps the writer focus on the most appropriate ideas to include.

There are many specific purposes for writing, but they will usually fall within one of these three main categories.

Purpose	Examples
to explain	expository essay, how-to paper, cause-and-effect explanation, comparison and contrast essay
to convince or persuade	letter to the editor, persuasive essay, petition to city council
to tell a story	fable, fairy tale, short story, novel, personal narrative, anecdote

Audience

Writers pay attention to their **audience**, or readers, too. They need to consider what their audience may already know, so they can focus on ideas and content that are new and interesting. An audience may consist of teachers, parents or other family members, classmates, younger children, community members, or even online readers.

Before you begin writing, ask yourself the following questions:
• Who will read what I write?
• What do I know about my audience?
• Why do I want my audience to care about my writing?
• What do I have to say to my audience?
• Am I writing opinions or facts?
• Will my writing be funny or serious, happy or sad?

✚ ORGANIZATION

Organization is the way in which writers structure their ideas and content. Writers need to organize their ideas. Without organization, the ideas might seem like a random pile of puzzle pieces. Readers should not have to figure out which idea is most important or how the ideas connect. An organized paper clearly shows readers how one idea joins the next. As a result, readers understand how all the pieces fit together.

Before you can determine if a piece of writing is organized, you should be familiar with the organizational patterns writers may use. The most common patterns are listed below.
- **Chronological order** presents ideas, actions, or events in the order that they take place.
- **Spatial order** presents details and information according to location; for example, the writer describes something from near to far, top to bottom, inside to outside, or the reverse.
- **Order of importance** arranges ideas from the least to most important, or the reverse.
- **Logical order** groups related ideas together.

Usually a writer chooses one main organizational pattern for a paper, but he or she may use more than one. Sometimes there will be one organizational structure for the paper as a whole, and then the individual paragraphs will follow a different type of organization. The main pattern a writer chooses often depends on the purpose for writing.

For this purpose,	writers may use these organizational patterns:
Expository (to explain)	• *chronological order* to explain the steps in a process or retell historical events • *spatial order* to help readers picture the subject • *order of importance* to explain causes and effects • *logical order* to present groups of related facts or evidence
Persuasive (to convince)	• *order of importance* to present the most persuasive ideas first or last • *logical order* to group related ideas and supporting evidence together
Narrative (to tell a story)	• *chronological order* to tell events in the order that they happen • *spatial order* to help readers imagine an object or setting

Six Traits for Writing Success, Middle School

As you read a paper, you can try these strategies for identifying the organizational structure:

1. **Look for clue words, such as transitional words and phrases.** For example, transitional words such as *then*, *after*, and *finally* are usually used for chronological order. Words and phrases such as *next to*, *on top of*, *beside*, *to the left*, and *below* probably indicate that spatial order is being used.

2. **Identify the topic of each paragraph and see how the paragraphs relate to one another.** You may notice that the paragraphs show logical relationships, indicating a logical organizational structure. Or you may notice that each paragraph seems to have more impact than the paragraph before. This type of relationship would probably indicate that the writer has used order of importance to organize the paper.

3. **Map out the ideas in the text.** Creating a graphic organizer can help you see a paper's organizational structure. For example, a flow chart will reveal the chronological or cause-and-effect structure in a text. A Venn diagram (two intersecting circles) can illuminate the writer's use of comparison and contrast and help the reader understand logical order.

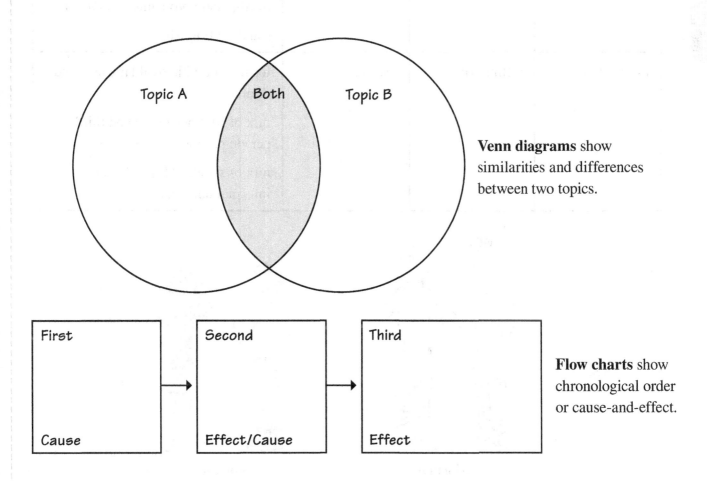

Venn diagrams
Topic A   Both   Topic B

Venn diagrams show similarities and differences between two topics.

First   Second   Third

Cause   Effect/Cause   Effect

Flow charts show chronological order or cause-and-effect.

VOICE

Voice is the way a piece of writing "sounds" to the reader. A writer uses his or her own style to "talk" to readers, and the voice reveals his or her feelings about both the topic and the audience. Voice allows the writer to connect as a person with the reader. Everyone has a natural voice, but good writers are able to tailor their voices to suit their purpose for writing, their topic, and their audience.

Purpose	Topic	Audience	Appropriate Voice
to inform or explain	walrus babies	fellow students	natural but not too casual third-person pronouns (*he/she/it*) standard English and scientific terms
to persuade	for constructing new bike paths	city council	formal and polite but assertive and serious third-person pronouns (*he/she/it*) standard English
to entertain	rafting trip	teacher	formal but with vivid language and drama mix of first-person (*I*) and third-person pronouns (*he/she/it*) mix of standard English and informal language

Informal

Formal

Choosing the right voice for a paper is similar to choosing the right clothes for the occasion.

WORD CHOICE

Word choice has a big effect on how a writer expresses his or her voice. Words are the building blocks of any piece of writing. The words a writer chooses help create a clear voice and engage the reader. Choosing just the right word is like landing an arrow right in the center of the target.

Word choice makes expository writing more precise, persuasive writing more convincing, and narrative writing more interesting. It helps readers to imagine a scene in a story or to understand the subtle points in a persuasive argument. Without thoughtful word choice, writing is imprecise and dull. Readers become bored or give up.

Before you can determine if a piece of writing contains effective word choices, you may want to review the following terms: **connotation and denotation, idiom, jargon, loaded language,** and **tired or clichéd language.**

• **Connotation and denotation:** The denotation of a word is its definition. The connotation is the feeling associated with the word. Since connotations often stir people's emotions, they can have powerful effects on a reader. Connotations also reveal the writer's attitude toward the subject.

Example: The word *mild* has the denotation of "gentle, not sharp or severe." The feeling associated with it is weakness. Its connotation can be negative or positive. For example, mild weather feels great after a cold winter, but a mild expression conveys a lack of interest.

• An **idiom** is a phrase or expression that means something different from the literal meanings of the words it contains. Idioms are informal. They are great for personal writing or in dialogues in fictional narratives, but they should be avoided in formal writing.

Examples: *Maria put up with the children.*
Don't get so bent out of shape about it.
I just don't get it.
John has a chip on his shoulder.
The test was a breeze.
The time flew by while we were shopping.

• **Jargon** is technical or specialized language that is used by a group of people who share the same profession, occupation, field of study, or hobby. Common words can be jargon. Their meanings can change in different contexts. Jargon works only if the writer knows that the audience will understand the meaning. Used properly, jargon conveys the writer's knowledge of a subject.

Examples: *Stock prices went down.*
                The soup requires chicken <u>stock</u>.
                The store needs fresh <u>stock</u>.

• **Loaded language** deliberately provokes a strong reaction from people and reveals a writer's bias. Loaded language works in persuasive writing, but it must be used carefully so as not to offend readers. In narratives, it can be used to show what a character is like.

Example: *Only <u>people of privilege</u> ride in first class on airplanes. The rest of us are <u>corralled</u> in coach <u>like cattle</u>.*

• **Tired or clichéd words** are phrases and words that have been used so much that they have lost their freshness. Clichés and overused words suggest a lack of imagination on the writer's part, so they should be avoided.

Examples: *The baby's face was <u>as red as a beet</u>.*
                She was an <u>eager beaver</u> during practice.
                It was the <u>straw that broke the camel's back</u>.
                Ah, <u>home, sweet home</u>.

≋ SENTENCE FLUENCY

Sentence fluency is how the sentences in a piece of writing flow together. Think of a tapestry. A tapestry maker weaves thousands of threads together to create a beautiful pattern or picture. Writing is like a tapestry, with sentences instead of threads. A good writer weaves the sentences together to show the flow of ideas in an interesting way. Unlike tapestry makers, however, writers have to construct their flowing "threads." They must build sentences that are both grammatically correct and interesting. Good writers use a mixture of short and long sentences, as well as sentences will start with phrases or clauses, to create a rhythm and style that will engage readers.

Before you can determine if a piece of writing has sentence fluency, you should review the following problems that can interfere with it: **sentence fragments**, **run-on sentences**, **stringy sentences**, **choppy sentences**, and **wordy sentences**.

- A **sentence fragment** is a group of words that has been capitalized and punctuated as if it were a complete sentence, but it may lack a subject, a verb, or both, or it may not express a complete thought.

Examples: *Finished his homework.* (lacks a subject)
Then he dinner. (lacks a verb)
For the whole family. (lacks a subject and verb)
Before Dad came home. (not a complete thought)

Sentence fragments interrupt sentence fluency and are grammatically incorrect. Readers must puzzle out the writer's meaning.

Better: *Toby finished his homework. Then he made dinner for the whole family before Dad came home.*

- **Run-on sentences** run two or more sentences together as if they were one.

Example: *People who want to adopt a puppy should visit a local animal shelter shelters always have puppies that need good homes.*

Run-ons are grammatically incorrect and confuse readers. They make it too difficult for a reader to tell where one idea ends and another begins.

Better: *People who want to adopt a puppy should visit a local animal shelter. Shelters always have puppies that need good homes.*

Sentence Fluency

- **Stringy sentences** have too many ideas strung together with conjunctions and transition words.

Example: *My grandmother dreamed of becoming a teacher, but she was poor, but then she won a scholarship, so she attended a college, and she found a job right away.*

Stringy sentences just go on and on, and they are confusing because the reader can't tell which idea is most important. Readers may also lose interest or "tune out" because they never get to "take a breath" and grasp the meaning.

Better: *My grandmother dreamed of becoming a teacher, but she was poor. Fortunately, she won a scholarship and was able to attend college. After she got her degree, she found a job right away.*

- **Choppy sentences** are very short. One or two very short sentences here and there can be effective at getting a reader's attention. However, a series of choppy sentences disrupts the flow of ideas and makes the writing sound boring.

Examples: *I love cheese. I like pickles. I eat cheese and pickle sandwiches. Some people think it's strange. They are my favorite.*

A series of short, choppy sentences disrupts the flow of ideas and does not tell which idea is most important.

Better: *I love cheese, and I also like pickles. In fact, I eat cheese and pickle sandwiches. Some people think it's strange, but they are my favorite.*

- **Wordy sentences** use more words than are necessary to express an idea.

Examples: *I was late for school because of the fact that I missed the bus. When I got to the very end of the book, I wrote my report.*

The extra words get in the reader's way. A reader may have to edit them out.

Better: *I was late for school because I missed the bus. When I finished the book, I wrote my report.*

Sentence Fluency

CONVENTIONS

Conventions are the agreed rules of paragraphing, usage, grammar, spelling, and punctuation that good writers follow. Conventions help writers make their meanings clear. Think how confusing it would be if people were allowed to make up their own rules of spelling, punctuation, and grammar.

This paragraph contains errors in conventions. Notice how difficult it is to read.

> *The game it begun normly enouh. the two gards from are team handle the ball good and made some good plays but we could not score as much the other team. No one knew how much the game was about to chang tho the whole crowd cheered when are new post playor maddy gerard enters the game in the middle of the first half.*

It is much easier to read the paragraph and grasp the meaning when the writer follows the rules of usage, punctuation, and spelling.

> *The game began normally enough. The two guards from our team handled the ball well and made some good plays, but we could not score as much as the other team. No one knew how much the game was about to change, though. The whole crowd cheered when our new post player, Maddy Gerard, entered the game in the middle of the first half.*

A writer should always edit and proofread a paper for mistakes in conventions because even small mistakes can distract or confuse a reader. You want your readers to focus on your words and ideas, not on problems with your spelling or usage. Don't let convention errors slip by. Use a checklist like this one to help you catch them.

Proofreading Checklist

Paragraphing

_____ Is each paragraph indented?

_____ Does each paragraph focus on just one main idea?

_____ Does the paragraph break in a logical place? (If not, where should it break?)

Grammar and Usage

_____ Does every sentence have both a subject and a verb?

_____ Do the subject(s) and verb(s) in each sentence agree?

_____ Are the correct forms and tenses of verbs used?

_____ Do pronouns agree with their antecedents?

_____ Are the forms of personal pronouns used correctly?

_____ Are there any double negatives? (If so, how should they be corrected?)

Punctuation and Capitalization

_____ Does each sentence end with correct punctuation?

_____ Are commas and semicolons used correctly?

_____ Are proper nouns capitalized?

_____ Does each sentence or direct quotation begin with a capital letter?

_____ Are apostrophes used correctly to indicate possession or missing letters?

Spelling

_____ Are words that sound alike but are spelled differently spelled correctly?

_____ Are commonly misspelled words spelled correctly?

_____ Are words with suffixes and prefixes spelled correctly?

_____ Are people's names, place names, and other proper nouns spelled correctly?

Just in case you find convention errors in the papers you read, use the editing and proofreading marks shown below to make corrections.

Symbols for Editing and Proofreading

Symbol	Example	Meaning of Symbol
≈	at Emerson lake	Capitalize a lowercase letter.
/	a gift from my Aunt	Lowercase a capital letter.
∧	costs ∧ cents (thirty)	Insert a missing word, letter, or puncuation mark.
⌐	near their house (our)	Replace something.
℘	What time is is it?	Leave out a word, letter, or punctuational mark.
∽	redjeved	Change the order of the letters.
¶	¶The third effect is...	Begin a new paragraph.
⊙	Please sit down⊙	Add a period.
∧	Yes∧ I heard you.	Add a comma.

INTEGRATING THE SIX TRAITS INTO THE WRITING PROCESS
The Writing Process

Writing is a way to share your ideas with others. The writing process helps you move step by step from a blank sheet of paper to an interesting piece of writing. The writing process gives you many opportunities to improve your writing. You can move back and forth as necessary to make your writing the best that it can be. For example, if you are in the middle of writing your paper but discover that you need more ideas, you can go back to prewriting and find some more ideas.

The writing process has four main stages: Prewriting, Writing, Revising and Evaluating, and Publishing and Presenting.

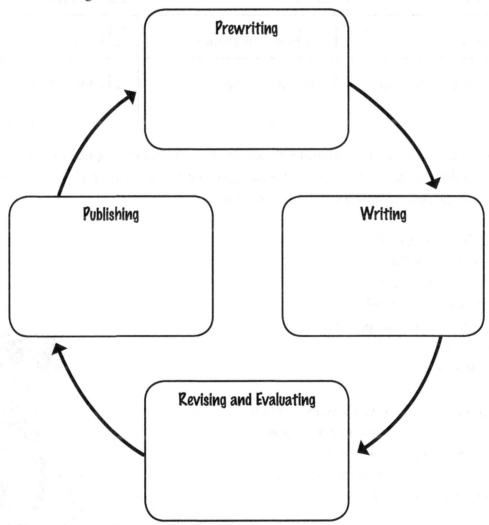

Stage 1: Prewriting

The first step of prewriting is to consider your purpose, audience, and genre.

Purpose: Why am I writing?	**Audience:** Who are my readers?	**Genre:** Which format will best suit my purpose and audience?
☐ to inform or explain	☐ classmates	☐ expository essay
☐ to persuade	☐ teachers	☐ persuasive essay
☐ to tell a story	☐ friends	☐ narrative essay
☐ to describe	☐ community members	☐ letter
☐ to express thoughts and feelings	☐ family members	☐ a short story

The next step is to choose a topic and explore what you know about that topic. You may find it helpful to brainstorm a list of ideas or to use graphic organizers to get your ideas on paper. See the following pages for helpful graphic organizers for recording ideas:

• Clustering: Word Web, p. 90
• Brainstorming: Freewriting, p. 91
• Identifying the Main Idea, p. 92
• Cause and Effect Chain, p. 93
• Personal Narrative Story Map, p. 94
• Pros and Cons, p. 95
• Stating an Opinion, p. 96

The last step is to organize your ideas and begin to plan your writing. You may want to outline your ideas or use graphic organizers to organize your thoughts. See the following pages for helpful graphic organizers for organizing ideas:

• Flow Chart: Chronological Order, p. 97
• Organizing Your Reasons, p. 98
• Organizing Reasons by Order of Importance, p. 99
• Using an Outline, p. 100

Stage 2: Writing

Writing, or drafting, is the stage where you express your main ideas clearly, support those ideas, and follow a plan of organization, adjusting the plan as needed to make meaning clear. In this stage, you're getting your ideas down on paper. Remember that a draft doesn't need to be perfect. You will refine your draft in the next stage.

Each writer has a slightly different way of drafting a paper. Some people write quickly, going with the flow of their ideas. Others draft slowly, carefully thinking about each sentence and paragraph they write. Trust your own way and do what works best for you.

You will want to keep the following basic guidelines in mind during the writing stage:

• Use your prewriting notes and your organizational plan to guide you as you write your first draft.
• If you come up with new ideas as you write, go ahead and include them if you think they will fit with the plan. You can always take them out later if they do not work well.
• Don't worry too much about grammar and spelling errors while you are drafting. You can correct those later.

Stage 3: Revising and Evaluating

The revising and evaluating stage may be the most important one in the process of writing a paper. It is where you figure out if your ideas, organization, and style are working and if you are communicating your ideas clearly.

In this stage, you should read your writing carefully to be sure it makes sense. You may find that you need to rearrange ideas or add or remove details to make your writing stronger. Consider reading your writing aloud or having someone else review your writing and provide feedback.

In addition, you should also be looking for any mistakes in grammar, usage, or mechanics.

• Revise any sentence fragments or run-on sentences.
• Fix mistakes in subject-verb agreement or pronoun agreement.
• Capitalize and use punctuation marks correctly.
• Correct any misspellings.

Stage 4: Publishing and Presenting

Publishing is the stage in the writing process where you make your paper ready for your actual readers. You can present your writing to your teacher, to your classmates, to your friends or family, or to the community. You can read it orally, post it on a Web site, or make it into a book, poster, or flyer.

A published paper should have a clean, pleasant appearance and should not contain visual elements that may distract the reader. Use the checklist below to make sure that your paper looks its best.

Checklist for Publication/Presentation

√ If your paper is handwritten, your letters are consistently and clearly formed, spacing is reasonable and uniform, and the words are easy to see and read.

√ If you have typed your paper using a word-processing program, your letters and words appear in a font and size that is easy to read.

√ There is a balance of white space (margins, spaces between words and paragraphs) and text on the page that allows the reader to focus on the text.

√ Any titles, subheadings, page numbers, bullets, and other graphics are the appropriate size and boldness. They help readers follow the flow of ideas. They do not distract readers from the words or the message of the text.

The Writing Process and the Six Traits

Good writers already use all six traits of writing—ideas, organization, voice, word choice, sentence structure, and conventions—as they prepare their papers. As you move through the writing process, use the six traits to shape and refine your writing. Some traits, such as ideas and content, organization, and voice, are useful in all four stages of writing. Other traits are mostly useful in the later stages to help you fine-tune your writing and produce an error-free publication.

- In the prewriting stage, you can focus mostly on ideas and content and begin thinking about organizational strategies.
- In the writing stage, you shift your focus more to content, organization, and voice. You may also be thinking about word choice and sentence structure, but these will not be your main focus.
- During the revising and evaluating stage, you make sure that your ideas and organizational strategies are sound. You also refine your voice and your word choices and revise your sentence structures to improve the style, rhythm, and clarity of your writing.
- As you prepare to publish your writing, you concentrate on sentence structures and correcting any writing convention errors.

Prewriting: Students think about their ideas and organization strategies. Graphic organizers or outlines are helpful.

Writing: Students shift focus to content, organization, and voice. They begin writing their papers.

Revising and Evaluating: Students review their papers to make sure ideas and organizational structures are sound. Self-Evaluation checklists are helpful.

Publishing and Presenting: Students make final edits and present their final papers.

At-a-Glance: The Six Traits of Writing and the Writing Process

SIX TRAITS	WRITING PROCESS			
	Prewriting	Writing	Revising and Evaluating	Publishing and Presenting
IDEAS AND CONTENT	Explore ideas and choose a topic. Gather ideas and details to develop the topic. Evaluate ideas.	Develop sentences and paragraphs that explain and elaborate on the ideas.	Evaluate and revise the content of the piece using **Guidelines for Self-Evaluation** found in the Writing Workshops.	Reflect on the completed piece. Consider, for example, how to approach a similar piece next time.
ORGANIZATION	Develop a thesis, opinion statement, or controlling idea. Organize the ideas and details into a coherent structure.	Decide how to introduce the piece effectively. State the thesis or controlling idea. Organize the piece so that it is coherent. Conclude the piece so that it has a sense of closure.	Evaluate and revise the organization of the piece using **Guidelines for Self-Evaluation** found in the Writing Workshops.	
VOICE	Think about audience, purpose, and tone.	Include cues that signal tone and make the audience aware of the piece's purpose. Connect with readers using a natural but appropriate writer's voice.	Evaluate the content of the piece using **Guidelines for Self-Evaluation** found in the Writing Workshops. Refine the style of the piece so that it suits the audience and purpose and conveys the writer's voice.	Publish the piece for its intended audience.

SIX TRAITS	WRITING PROCESS			
	Prewriting	**Writing**	**Revising and Evaluating**	**Publishing and Presenting**
WORD CHOICE		Use language effectively to convey ideas. Use precise words with the appropriate connotations. Avoid jargon, clichés, and loaded language.	Evaluate and revise the content of the piece using **Guidelines for Self-Evaluation** in the Writing Workshops. Revise word choices to give the piece the best possible impact on the audience.	
SENTENCE FLUENCY		Use effective transitions between sentences. Write clear sentences with varied structures.	Evaluate and revise the content of the piece using **Guidelines for Self-Evaluation** in the Writing Workshops. Refine flow and rhythm of sentences. Fix run-ons and sentence fragments. Revise to avoid wordy, choppy, and stringy sentences.	Identify and correct errors in sentence construction.
CONVENTIONS				Use the **Proofreading Checklist** to catch and correct errors in spelling, capitalization, punctuation, and grammar.

PART TWO

Using the Six Traits to Evaluate Writing

SIX TRAITS RUBRIC: IDEAS AND CONTENT

As you read others' papers, use the rubric below to evaluate each writer's ideas and content. (A score of 5 is the highest; a score of 1 is the lowest.)

Score 5	It's Crystal Clear!
A Score 5 paper is clear, focused, and interesting. It presents relevant and concrete details that catch and maintain the reader's interest and support a clear main idea, theme, or story line.	√ The topic is clearly focused—neither too broad nor too narrow—for a paper of its kind. √ The ideas are original, interesting, and creative. √ The writer draws from personal experience or knowledge. √ Key details are insightful and well chosen; they are not obvious, predictable, or clichéd. √ The development of the topic is thorough and logical; the writer anticipates and answers the reader's questions. √ Supporting details are accurate and relevant; every detail contributes to the whole.
Score 3	**Close—It's Getting There.**
A Score 3 paper develops the topic in a general or basic way. Although clear, the ideas in the paper are routine and lack insight.	√ The topic is underdeveloped, but readers can still understand the writer's purpose and predict how ideas will develop. √ Supporting details are present but can be vague and do not help illustrate the main idea or theme; the writer refers to his or her own experience or knowledge but often fails to push beyond the obvious to more specific ideas. √ Ideas are understandable but not detailed, elaborated upon, or personalized; the writer's ideas do not reveal deep comprehension of the topic or of the writing task. √ The writer does not stray from the topic, but the ideas remain general, forcing readers to rely on what they already know to make sense of the paper; more information is needed to create a complete picture.
Score 1	**Hmm. What Is the Writer Trying to Say?**
A Score 1 paper fails to exhibit any clear purpose or main idea. The reader must infer a coherent and meaningful message from scattered details and incomplete observations.	√ The writer appears not to have decided on a topic or main idea; the paper reads like a rough draft or brainstorming notes; it is full of random thoughts. √ The thesis is a vague statement about the topic or a restatement of a prompt, with little or no support, detail, or insight. √ Information is limited and spotty; readers must make inferences to make connections or to identify any organizational pattern. √ The text is rambling and repetitious; ideas are underdeveloped; the paper is too short. √ The paper lacks subordination of ideas; every idea and detail seems equally weighted; ideas are not tied to an overarching thesis or theme.

Evaluating Ideas and Content

Read the excerpt from a paper below and one reader's comments. The reader has focused on how the writer deals with main idea, details, purpose, and audience. The comments suggest that the writer is on target with main idea, purpose, and audience but not with details.

Although she was not an elected official herself, Dolley Payne Madison, the wife of President James Madison, was an important historical figure. She had a significant influence on the politics of her day and on the history of the United States. Born in Guilford County, North Carolina, in 1768, she grew up in Virginia and married her first husband, a lawyer named John Todd, Jr., in 1790. About a year after Todd's death in 1793, she remarried Congressman James Madison, an outspoken leader, political writer, and future president.

It was James Madison, along with Alexander Hamilton and John Jay, who authored the famous Federalist papers, a series of letters that spelled out the Federalist philosophy underlying the U.S. Constitution.

> The main idea—that Dolley Madison is important—is clearly stated.

> Hmm. These details are about her life, not about her importance.

> These details are about James. Need more details about Dolley.

You can tell that a paper has good ideas when you . . .
- get the writer's message (the most important idea) right away
- can easily spot and understand the main idea, theme, or story line
- know the writer's purpose for writing
- are interested in what the writer has to say
- pay attention to and can remember the paper's details

When you evaluate another student's paper, use the following questions to guide you:
- What is the writer trying to say?
- What is the most important piece of information?
- Do the details support the ideas?
- Are the details interesting and memorable?

SIX TRAITS RUBRIC: ✦ ORGANIZATION

As you read others' papers, use the rubric below to evaluate each writer's organization.
(A score of 5 is the highest; a score of 1 is the lowest.)

Score 5	Yes! I Can See Where This Is Going.
A Score 5 paper uses organizational patterns to clearly communicate a central idea or story line. The order of information draws the reader effortlessly through the text.	√ The paper employs a logical and effective sequence of ideas. √ The paper contains both an attention-grabbing introduction and a satisfying conclusion. √ The pacing is carefully controlled; the writer slows down to provide explanation or elaboration when appropriate and increases the pace when necessary. √ Transitions make clear connections and cue the reader to specific relationships between ideas. √ The organizational structure is appropriate to the writer's purpose and audience. √ If present, the title sums up the central idea of the paper in a fresh and thoughtful way.
Score 3	**Close—Wait, I Think I Get It.**
A Score 3 paper is reasonably strong; it enables readers to move forward without too much confusion.	√ The paper has an introduction and a conclusion. However, the introduction may not be engaging, and the conclusion may not knit together all the paper's ideas. √ The sequence is logical but predictable and therefore not very compelling. √ The sequence may not consistently support the paper's ideas; readers may reorder sections mentally or provide transitions as they read. √ Pacing is reasonably well done, although the writer may move ahead too quickly or linger over unimportant ideas. √ Transitions between ideas may be unclear. √ If present, the title may be dull or lacking insight.
Score 1	**Hmm. I'm a Little Lost.**
A Score 1 paper fails to exhibit a sense of purpose or writing strategy; ideas, details, or events seem to be cobbled together without any internal structure or flow.	√ The sequence is broken; one idea or event does not logically follow another; lack of organizational structure, such as clear paragraph breaks, makes it difficult for readers to understand the progression of ideas or events. √ The paper lacks both a clear introduction to guide readers and a conclusion that sums up ideas at the end. √ Pacing is halting or inconsistent; the writer appears not to know when to slow down or speed up the pace. √ Transitions between ideas are confusing or absent. √ If present, the title does not accurately reflect the content of the paper.

Evaluating Organization

Read the excerpt from a paper below and one reader's comments about its organizational structure. The reader has focused on how the ideas fit together. The reader's comments suggest that the writer needs to organize the ideas more logically.

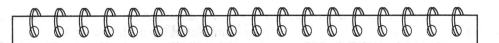

> Some people believe that machines may one day be as smart as humans. They point to computers as examples of artificial intelligence. Indeed, computers can do things that humans can do. Others, however, maintain that we will never have true artificial intelligence. But in fact, computers can do many things we can't, such as beat a Russian chess master at his own game, as the IBM computer Deep Blue did in 1997. On the other hand, computers don't really think. They may spell-check a paper quickly, but they can't understand context. As a result, they can't proofread a paper as thoughtfully as an editor. Most computers today would not pass the Turing Test, a series of questions answered by both a computer and a live person. If both answer the question the same way, the computer passes as intelligent.

Oh, I get it. The writer is comparing ideas about computer intelligence. Not clear, though.

This paragraph has too many different ideas. I can't follow.

The last two sentences do not fit here. Logically, they should be in a separate paragraph.

You can tell that a paper has a clear organizational structure when you . . .
- can see connections among the writer's ideas
- can concentrate on the ideas because the connections are clear
- feel that the writer is in control of the way ideas are presented
- feel that the writing has exactly the right pace
- can go back and find information easily because it is logically presented

When you evaluate another student's paper, use the following questions to guide you:
- How are the ideas in the paper organized?
- Does the writer's choice of organizational pattern suit the material?
- Can you see the connections among ideas, or do you feel confused?
- Would a change in the way ideas are presented make the paper better?

SIX TRAITS RUBRIC: VOICE

As you read others' papers, use the rubric below to evaluate writer's voice.
(A score of 5 is the highest; a score of 1 is the lowest.)

Score 5	Yes! I Can Really Hear You.
A Score 5 paper is engaging and conveys the writer's awareness of audience and purpose.	√ The tone of the writing is appropriate for the purpose and audience of the paper. √ The reader is aware of and feels connected to a real person behind the text; if appropriate, the writer takes risks in revealing a personal dimension throughout the piece. √ If the paper is expository or persuasive, the writer shows a strong connection to the topic and explains why readers should care about the issue. √ If the paper is narrative, the point of view is sincere, interesting, and compelling.
Score 3	**Close. Try Again With Feeling.**
A Score 3 paper is reasonably genuine but does not reveal any excitement or connection with the issue; the resulting paper is pleasant but not truly engaging.	√ The writer offers generalities instead of personal insights; as a result, the writing feels impersonal. √ The writer uses neutral language and a flat tone. √ The writer communicates in an earnest and pleasing manner yet takes no risks; the reader does not feel inspired or engaged. √ Expository or persuasive writing does not reveal the writer's engagement with the topic; there is no attempt to build credibility with the audience. √ Narrative writing fails to reveal a fresh or individual perspective.
Score 1	**Hmm. I Can Barely Hear You.**
A Score 1 paper is mechanical or wooden. The writer appears indifferent to the topic and the audience.	√ The writer shows no concern with the audience; the voice may be inappropriate for the intended reader. √ The development of the topic is so limited that no identifiable point of view is present, or the writing is so short that it offers little but a general introduction of the topic. √ The writer seems to speak in a monotone, using a voice that suppresses all excitement about the message or topic. √ Although the writing may communicate on a functional level, it is ordinary and takes no risks. √ Expository or persuasive writing may lack accurate information or use overly technical language. Narrative writing may lack a point of view and fail to inspire interest.

Voice

Evaluating Voice

Read the first excerpt from a persuasive paper below and one reader's comments about it. The reader has focused on the writer's voice. The comment suggests that the writer needs to fix his or her voice.

The language is informal, but the topic is serious. The voice is too casual.

Parks should be safe. People enjoying the parks should not have to be stressin' about loose dogs that may mosey up to them. Owners of unleashed dogs are usually somewhere else in the park yakking with their friends instead of paying attention. They are too far away to deal with their lousy dogs. This happens every day at the park next to my house. It probably happens in other parks too, and it's a drag because it messes up the park for everybody.

Identify four examples of informal language from the paragraph and rewrite using formal language.

Example: *lousy dogs – misbehaving dogs*

_____

_____

_____

_____

_____

_____

_____

Now read the revised version and think about how the new voice has improved the writing.

Parks should be safe. People enjoying the parks should not have to worry about loose dogs that may approach them. Owners of unleashed dogs are usually somewhere else in the park and are unable to effectively control their dogs if they misbehave. This happens every day at the park next to my house, and it is a shame because it ruins the park for everybody.

Formal language suits the serious topic better.

Use of first person is okay; it informs and sounds formal, polite.

You can tell that a paper has a clear and appropriate voice when you . . .
• feel that the voice "sounds" right
• are aware of and feel connected to the person behind the text
• understand the writer's connection to the topic
• are not distracted by inappropriate language or feelings

When you evaluate another student's paper, use the following questions to guide you:
• Does the writer's voice sound right?
• Does the writer's voice suit his or her purpose and audience?
• Is the writer using his or her voice to connect with me?
• Does the writer seem interested in the topic and in me?

"If my topic is serious, my voice should be too."

Voice

SIX TRAITS RUBRIC: WORD CHOICE

As you read others' papers, use the rubric below to evaluate writer's voice.
(A score of 5 is the highest; a score of 1 is the lowest.)

Score 5	Yes! Your Words Come Through Loud and Clear.
In a Score 5 paper, words are precise, engaging, and natural. They convey the writer's message in an interesting and effective way.	√ All words are specific and appropriate. In all instances, the writer has taken care to choose the right words or phrases. √ The paper's language is natural, not overdone; it never shows a lack of control. Clichés and jargon are rarely used. √ The paper contains energetic verbs; precise nouns and modifiers provide clarity. √ The writer uses vivid words and phrases, including sensory details; such language creates distinct images in the reader's mind.
Score 3	**Close—With a Little Polish Your Words Will Shine.**
Despite its lack of flair, the writing in a Score 3 paper gets the message across because it is functional and clear.	√ Words are correct and generally adequate but lack originality or precision. √ Familiar words and phrases do not grab the reader's interest or imagination. Occasional use of lively verbs and phrases perks things up, but the language does not consistently sparkle. √ Attempts at engaging or academic language may seem showy or overdone. √ The writing contains passive verbs and basic nouns and adjectives, and it lacks precise adverbs.
Score 1	**Hmm. I Don't Understand What You Mean.**
The limited vocabulary in a Score 1 paper prevents readers from understanding the writer's message. The writer's struggle for words keeps readers from making connections.	√ Vague language communicates an imprecise or incomplete message or understanding of the topic. The reader feels confused and unsure of the writer's purpose. √ Words are used incorrectly. In addition, frequent misuse of parts of speech limits readers' comprehension. √ Excessive repetition distracts readers from the message. √ The writing overuses jargon or clichés.

Word Choice

Evaluating Word Choice

Read the excerpt from the paper below and one reader's comments. The reader has focused on the writer's choice of words. The comments point out where word choice is effective—and where it is not.

"Smug" has negative connotations. The writer doesn't like smug detectives.

Loaded language—you can tell that the writer is biased in favor of the hard-boiled mysteries.

A uniquely American creation in literature is the hard-boiled detective story. Whether in the form of a novel, a short story, a movie, or a television show, the key element in a hard-boiled detective mystery is the characterization. All of the characters in a hard-boiled detective story should be more or less realistic. The forerunners of hard-boiled detective stories were the English drawing-room mysteries. Typically, in these stories, a smug sleuth would brilliantly solve a mysterious murder in a manor house without even breaking a sweat. Drawing-room mysteries are as soothing as a cup of herbal tea and just as stimulating, whereas hard-boiled mysteries are like a punch in the arm.

"Hard-boiled" is jargon. Mystery readers know what it means—dark, realistic mysteries.

"Breaking a sweat" is a cliché. The writer should try "breaking a fingernail."

Word Choice

You can tell that a paper has solid word choices when you . . .
• feel that each word is specific and appropriate
• can say that the language feels natural, not overdone
• do not notice any clichés, jargon, or inappropriate language
• feel engaged by the writing
• are not distracted by words that are confusing or used incorrectly

When you evaluate another student's paper, use the following questions to guide you:
• Why did the writer choose a certain word?
• Would another word have worked better in that sentence?
• Does the language sound natural and appropriate?
• What feelings or ideas does the writer's choice of words suggest?

SIX TRAITS RUBRIC: ≋ SENTENCE FLUENCY

As you read others' papers, use the rubric below to evaluate writer's voice.
(A score of 5 is the highest; a score of 1 is the lowest.)

Score 5	Yes! The Sentences Really Flow.
Sentences in a Score 5 paper are thoughtfully constructed, and sentence structure is varied throughout. When read aloud, the writing is fluent and rhythmic.	√ The writer constructs sentences so that meaning is clear to the reader. √ Sentences vary in length and in structure. √ Varied sentence beginnings add interest and clarity. √ The writing has a steady rhythm; the reader is able to read the text effortlessly without confusion or stumbling. √ Dialogue, if used, is natural. Any fragments are used purposefully and contribute to the paper's style. √ Thoughtful connectives and transitions between sentences reveal how the paper's ideas work together.
Score 3	**Close—But I Feel As Though I'm Drifting Off Course.**
Text of a Score 3 paper maintains a steady rhythm, but the reader may find it flat or mechanical rather than fluent or musical.	√ Sentences are usually grammatical and unified, but they are routine rather than artful. The writer has not paid a great deal of attention to how the sentences sound. √ There is some variation in sentence length and structure as well as in sentence beginnings. Not all sentences are constructed exactly the same way. √ The reader may have to search for transitional words and phrases that show how sentences relate to one another. Sometimes, such context clues are entirely absent when they should be present. √ Although sections of the paper invite expressive oral reading, the reader may also encounter many stilted or awkward sections.
Score 1	**Hmm. I'm a Little Lost.**
Readers of a Score 1 paper will encounter challenges in reading the choppy or confusing text; meaning may be significantly obscured by the errors in sentence construction.	√ The sentences do not "hang together." They are run-on, incomplete, monotonous, or awkward. √ Phrasing often sounds too singsong, not natural. The paper does not allow for expressive oral reading. √ Nearly all the sentences begin the same way, and they may all follow the same pattern (e.g., subject-verb-object). The end result may be a monotonous repetition of sounds. √ Endless connectives or a complete lack of connectives creates a confused muddle of language.

Six Traits for Writing Success, Middle School

Evaluating Sentence Fluency

Read the excerpt from the paper below and one reader's comments about it. The reader has focused on the paper's sentence fluency. The comments point out where sentences flow well and where they do not.

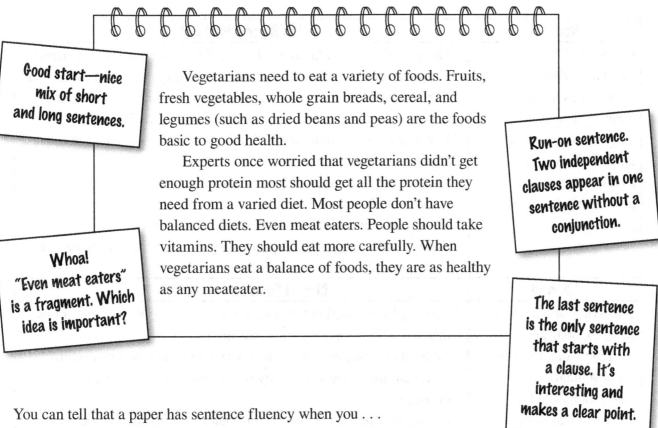

> Good start—nice mix of short and long sentences.

> Whoa! "Even meat eaters" is a fragment. Which idea is important?

Vegetarians need to eat a variety of foods. Fruits, fresh vegetables, whole grain breads, cereal, and legumes (such as dried beans and peas) are the foods basic to good health.

Experts once worried that vegetarians didn't get enough protein most should get all the protein they need from a varied diet. Most people don't have balanced diets. Even meat eaters. People should take vitamins. They should eat more carefully. When vegetarians eat a balance of foods, they are as healthy as any meateater.

> Run-on sentence. Two independent clauses appear in one sentence without a conjunction.

> The last sentence is the only sentence that starts with a clause. It's interesting and makes a clear point.

You can tell that a paper has sentence fluency when you . . .
• understand the writer's meaning and see connections between ideas
• understand which idea is most important
• feel engaged by the writing
• appreciate the rhythm and style of the sentences
• notice the variety of sentence beginnings and lengths

When you evaluate another student's paper, use the following questions to guide you:
• Does the writing feel natural as it flows from one idea to the next?
• Are the sentences interesting and grammatically correct?
• Do the sentences express ideas and make clear connections?

SIX TRAITS RUBRIC: CONVENTIONS

As you read others' papers, use the rubric below to evaluate writer's voice.
(A score of 5 is the highest; a score of 1 is the lowest.)

Score 5	It's Nearly Perfect!
In a Score 5 paper, standard writing conventions are used correctly and in a way that aids the reader's understanding. Any errors tend to be minor; the piece is nearly ready for publication.	√ Paragraphing is regular and enhances the organization of the paper. √ Grammar and usage are correct and add clarity to the text as a whole. Sometimes the writer may manipulate conventions in a controlled way—especially grammar and spelling—for stylistic effect. √ Punctuation is accurate; it enables the reader to move through the text with understanding and ease. √ The writer's understanding of capitalization rules is evident throughout the paper. √ Most words, even difficult ones, are spelled correctly. √ The writing is long and complex enough to show the writer using a wide range of convention skills successfully.
Score 3	**Close. I Found a Few Errors.**
The writer of a Score 3 paper exhibits an awareness of a limited set of standard writing conventions and uses them to enhance the paper's readability. Some errors distract and confuse readers. Moderate editing is required before publication.	√ Paragraphs are used but may begin in the wrong places, or sections that should be separate paragraphs are run together. √ Conventions may not always be correct; however, problems with grammar and usage are usually not serious enough to distort meaning. √ End marks are usually correct, but other punctuation marks, such as commas, apostrophes, semicolons, and parentheses, may be missing or wrong. √ Common words are usually spelled correctly. √ Most words are capitalized correctly, but the writer's command of capitalization skills is inconsistent.
Score 1	**Hmm. I'm Distracted by Too Many Errors.**
In a Score 1 paper, there are errors in spelling, punctuation, grammar and usage, and paragraphing that seriously impede the reader's comprehension. Extensive editing is required for publication.	√ Paragraphing is missing, uneven, or too frequent. Most of the paragraphs do not reinforce or support the organizational structure of the paper. √ Errors in grammar and usage are very common and distracting; such errors also affect the paper's meaning. √ Punctuation, including end punctuation, is often missing or incorrect. √ Even common words are frequently misspelled. √ Capitalization is haphazard or reveals the writer's understanding of only the simplest rules. √ The paper must be read once just to decode the language and then again to capture the paper's meaning.

Evaluating the Use of Conventions

Read the excerpt from the paper below and one reader's corrections. The reader has focused on the writer's use of conventions.

>   There
> Their are several types of prejudice, such as social,
>   is
> political and racial prejudices. Everyone, are prejudiced
>
> against some sort of thing. It might be food, cars,
>
> races of people, etc. I believe to overcome prejudice
>
> is to not show your feelings towards something you
>
> are prejudiced about. If you are prejudiced against
>
> someone's nationality without even personally meeting
>
> this person, I think that is wrong, or if one person
>
> is a certain race, and they commit a crime, don't
>
> never think everyone of that race is exactly like that.
>   his or her
> Everyone has, their own personality. I believe that you
>
> should welcome everyone instead of saying you don't
>
> like someone because of nationality or race.

You can tell that a paper has correct conventions when you . . .

• do not see any convention errors

• feel that the writer's meaning is clear and not affected by small errors

• feel that the writer has excellent control of conventions

When you evaluate another student's paper, use the following questions to guide you:

• Do I notice any convention errors?

• Do the convention errors interfere with my understanding?

• Does the writer need to brush up on the rules of grammar, usage, or punctuation?

• Does the writer need to remember to use a dictionary or a spell-checker?

Conventions

SIX TRAITS: AT-A-GLANCE RUBRIC

As you read others' papers, use this At-a-Glance rubric to evaluate writer's use of all of the six traits. (A score of 5 is the highest; a score of 1 is the lowest.)

IDEAS AND CONTENT	ORGANIZATION	VOICE
5 The paper is clear and focused, with ideas that engage the reader. √ The topic is clearly focused for a paper of its kind. √ The ideas are original, interesting, and creative. √ The writer draws from personal experience. √ Key details are insightful and well chosen. √ The development of the topic is thorough and logical. √ Supporting details are accurate and relevant.	**5 The organizational structure suits the content and connects ideas.** √ The paper employs a logical and effective sequence of ideas. √ The paper contains both an introduction and a conclusion. √ The pacing is carefully controlled. √ Transitions make clear connections and cue the reader to relationships between ideas. √ The organizational structure is appropriate to the writer's purpose and audience.	**5 The writer's personality is clear and engaging.** √ The tone of the writing is appropriate for the purpose and audience of the paper. √ The reader is aware of and feels connected to a real person behind the text. √ If the paper is expository or persuasive, the writer shows a strong connection to the topic and tells why readers should care. √ If the paper is narrative, the point of view is sincere, interesting, and compelling.
3 The ideas are vague and not fully thought out. √ The topic is underdeveloped, but readers can still understand the writer's purpose. √ Supporting details are present but can be vague and do not help illustrate the main idea or theme. √ Ideas are understandable but not detailed, elaborated upon, or personalized. √ The ideas remain general; more information is needed to create a complete picture.	**3 The organization is clear, but readers may get confused.** √ The paper has an introduction and a conclusion. √ The sequence is logical but predictable and therefore not very compelling. √ The sequence may not consistently support the paper's ideas. √ Pacing is reasonably well done. √ Transitions between ideas may be unclear.	**3 The writer is sincere but not completely engaged.** √ The writer offers generalities that feel impersonal. √ The writer uses neutral language and a slightly flattened tone. √ The writer communicates in an earnest and pleasing manner yet takes no risks. √ Expository or persuasive writing does not reveal an engagement with the topic. √ Narrative writing fails to reveal a fresh or individual perspective.
I The paper lacks clear ideas and purpose. √ The paper reads like a rough draft or brainstorming notes. √ The thesis is a vague statement about the topic or a restatement of a prompt, with little or no support or detail. √ Information is limited and spotty; readers must make inferences.	**I The paper fails to make connections and show the big picture.** √ One idea or event does not logically follow another; lack of organizational structure makes it difficult for readers to understand the progression of ideas or events. √ The paper lacks both a clear introduction and a conclusion. √ Pacing is halting or inconsistent. √ Transitions between ideas are confusing or absent.	**I The writer seems uninvolved in the topic and the reader.** √ The writer shows no concern with the audience. √ The writing lacks a point of view. √ The writer seems to speak in a monotone. √ The writing is ordinary and takes no risks. √ Expository or persuasive writing may lack accurate information. √ Narrative writing may lack a point of view and fail to interest.

WORD CHOICE	SENTENCE FLUENCY	CONVENTIONS
5 The words bring the paper to life and engage the reader. √ All words are specific and appropriate. The writer chooses the right words or phrases. √ The paper's language is natural and controlled. Clichés and jargon appear rarely. √ The paper contains energetic verbs; precise nouns and modifiers provide clarity. √ The writer uses vivid words and phrases, including sensory details.	**5 The sentences are varied and interesting.** √ The writer constructs sentences so that meaning is clear. √ Sentences vary in length and in structure. √ Varied sentence beginnings add interest and clarity. √ The reader is able to read the text effortlessly without confusion. √ Dialogue, if used, is natural. Fragments are used purposefully. √ Thoughtful connectives and transitions between sentences bring the ideas together.	**5 The writing is clear and uses correct spelling, punctuation, and grammar.** √ Paragraphing is regular and enhances the organization of the paper. √ Grammar and usage are correct and add clarity to the text. √ Punctuation is accurate. √ The writer understands the rules of capitalization. √ Most words, even difficult ones, are spelled correctly. √ The writing successfully shows a wide range of convention skills.
3 The language is clear but uninspired. √ Words are correct and adequate, not original or precise. √ Familiar words and phrases do not grab the reader's interest or imagination. The language does not consistently sparkle. √ Attempts at engaging language may seem showy. √ The writing contains passive verbs and basic nouns and adjectives, and it lacks precise adverbs.	**3 The sentences make sense, but the connections are not clear.** √ Sentences are usually grammatical, but they are routine rather than artful. √ There is some variation in sentence length and structure as well as in sentence beginnings. √ The reader may have to search for transitional words and phrases that show how sentences relate to one another. √ The reader may also encounter many stilted or awkward sections.	**3 Basic punctuation, grammar, and spelling are employed, but there are some mistakes.** √ Paragraphs are used but may begin in the wrong places. √ Conventions may not always be correct; however, problems are not serious enough to distort meaning. √ End marks are usually correct, but other punctuation marks, such as commas, apostrophes, semicolons, and parentheses, may be missing or wrong. √ Common words are usually spelled correctly.
1 The language is used incorrectly or ineffectively. √ Vague language communicates an incomplete message or understanding of the topic. The reader feels confused and unsure of the writer's purpose. √ Words are used incorrectly. √ Excessive repetition distracts readers from the message. √ The writing overuses jargon or clichés.	**1 The sentences are awkward and do not connect ideas.** √ The sentences do not "hang together"; they are run-on, incomplete, or awkward. √ Phrasing often sounds too singsong, not natural. √ Nearly all the sentences begin the same way, and they may all follow the same pattern (e.g., subject-verb-object). √ Endless connectives or a lack of connectives creates a confused muddle of language.	**1 The paper contains many errors that interfere with the meaning.** √ Paragraphing is missing, uneven, or too frequent. √ Errors in grammar and usage are common and distracting and affect the paper's meaning. √ Punctuation, including end marks, is often missing or incorrect. √ Even common words are frequently misspelled. √ Capitalization reveals the writer's understanding of only the simplest rules. √ The paper must be read once just to decode the language and then again to capture the paper's meaning.

Six Traits for Writing Success, Middle School

EVALUATING AN EXPOSITORY ESSAY USING THE SIX WRITING TRAITS

Directions: A student responded to the expository prompt below. Read the student's essay and the completed evaluation on the next page. Then answer the questions that follow.

Expository Prompt *"I have a dream that my four little children will one day live in a nation where they will not be judged by the color of their skin but by the content of their character." Write an essay explaining what you think Dr. Martin Luther King, Jr. means in this quotation. You may use examples from real life, books, movies, or television shows.*

It does not matter what color people are, how they, dress, what kind of car they drive, or how big the house is in which they live. A person should be judged by his or her responsibility. A white man can have the same morals as a black man. Their principles can be identical. They can both be angels, or just as likely they can both be criminals.

A person's color does not gaurantee that his or her personality and demeanor will fit into a certain, forechosen category. Just because a person's skin color is white does not mean that he or she is a good person. Or that a black person is a criminal. Take the case of Ruben "Hurricane" Carter. He was convicted of murder and spent several years in prison based on absolutely no evidence of any kind. The all-white jury convicted him solely on the fact that he was black. He could have been the boxing champion of the world. Instead he was sent to prison where his health deteriorated. Literature provides us with many illustrations of racial stereotyping. For example, Tom Robinson, the main black character in To Kill a Mockingbird, was accused of a very serious crime against a white person. During the trial it became clear that the charges were not at all true. The defense lawyer, Atticus Finch, stated that Tom's only crime was to feel sorry for and to help a white person. In other words, Tom's real offense was the color of his skin.

Notes

A person should be judged based on his or her responsibility, clearheadedness, and ability to determine and do the right thing. A man cannot be juadged by the fact that he cannot walk, needs glasses to see, is not six feet tall, or needs a hearing aid. A man can only be judged by close examination of his scruples, morals, principles, and judgement. When a man is judged on unimportant qualities, it should be a crime. We will never forget the attempt by Nazi Germany to weed out people who were considered to be weak or flawed. Although the Nazis seemed superiour, they possessed the true flaws.

Martin Luther King, Jr. fought hard to instill this kind of thinking into his family and into everyone around him. He died fighting for this idea to be heard. He gave his life to try and teach the world about respect, decency, friendship, and most of all love between races. We should all try and learn from his words of wisdom.

Notes

One Reader's Evaluation

A reader used the six traits rubrics on pages 25–39 to evaluate the preceding expository essay. Below are her scores and comments.

Expository Essay: Six Trait Scores	
Trait	**Score**
Ideas and Content: The paper clearly responds to the prompt and stays focused on the topic of prejudice. The examples from life, history, and literature are accurate, interesting, and compelling. The writer has clear ideas about prejudice.	5
Organization: Overall, the organization is good. The essay has a clear introduction and conclusion. The writer could use more transitions to help readers follow the flow of examples.	4
Voice: The writer clearly feels strongly about the topic. I feel that the writer is clearly speaking in his or her own voice and is willing to take risks in expressing ideas.	5
Word Choice: Although the writer is earnest, his or her choice of words is often too general. Some words like "demeanor" and "scruples" fit nicely, but "forechosen" is a bit of a stretch. The writer uses "big idea" words that could be more specific.	3
Sentence Fluency: The sentence structure is varied, and there is an interesting rhythm that helps move readers through the paper. Some sentences have awkward or repetitive phrasing: ". . . based on absolutely no evidence of any kind."	4
Conventions: The writer demonstrates a fair understanding of conventions. Although there are some stray commas and spelling errors, they do not interfere with the writer's meaning.	5
Overall Comments:	
Overall I thought the paper was coherent, thoughtful, and engaging. I could tell the writer cared deeply about the message that prejudice is bad.	

> ***What's the Score?*** Even an excellent paper may not get 5's for every score. The point of scoring the traits is not to get an overall score or grade. It is to see which traits are strong for a writer and which need more work. This way the writer can improve the paper and also improve his or her writing on future assignments.

Name _____ Date _____

Your Turn

Now answer the questions below. Use the rubrics on pages 25–39 to figure out how you would score the essay on pages 40–41. How do your responses compare to the scores given by the reader on the previous page?

1. I do/ do not agree with the evaluator's score on the writer's ideas and content because

_____

_____

2. I do/ do not agree with the evaluator's score on the writer's organization because

_____

_____

3. I do/ do not agree with the evaluator's score on the writer's voice because

_____

_____

4. I do/ do not agree with the evaluator's score on the writer's word choice because

_____

_____

5. I do/ do not agree with the evaluator's score on the writer's sentence fluency because

_____

_____

6. I do/ do not agree with the evaluator's score on the writer's conventions because

_____

_____

7. If you were to give the essay different scores from the ones on page 42, what would they be?

_____

_____

PRACTICE EVALUATING AN EXPOSITORY ESSAY

Expository Essay: Read the prompt and the expository essay below. Then review the six traits rubrics on pages 25–39. Use the blank evaluation form that follows to score the writer's work.

Expository Prompt *Jeannette Rankin was the first woman ever elected to the United States Congress. She was a dedicated pacifist, a person who opposed war. She is famous for stating, "You can no more win a war than you can win an earthquake." Write an essay in which you explain what you think Rankin meant in this quotation. You may use examples from real life as well as from books, movies, or television shows.*

War and earthquakes are alike in many ways. I think Ms. Rankin is saying that war and earthquakes are alike in that they both produce the same results. Both of them end up with the same kinds of disasters and have a major impact on the world. When a war starts, no one is sure how it will end, but they know that the results are usually bad. Buildings are destroyed and people are killed. An earthquake is just like that because when it starts you have no idea when it will end, or what problems it will produce. But when it is over, it has caused a lot of damage. You really cannot win either way you look at it. Even if you win a war, many things are lost in the process.

War is like an earthquake in another way. Both of them are unpredictable. You never know when they are coming. Scientists study earthquakes and what causes them. But they still can't predict them very well. Earthquakes are happening every day in the world. Some of them you don't feel or hear about, but the ones you do hear about have the greatest impact on our lives. In America, the worst earthquakes happen in California, and their effects are all over the news—how many were killed or injured, what houses or buildings were lost, and which roads were destroyed.

Notes

Earthquakes and wars are also similar because they change people's lives. When wars are over, people have to rebuild their homes. If they or someone they loved was injured or killed, they also have to rebuild their lives. The same things happens with earthquakes. After an earthquake, people have to rebuild.

America has won a lot of wars in the past, but we lost so much in the process. Think of all the names carved into the walls of the Vietnam Memorial. Think of all the prisoners of war and what they went through. What about their families? You should not start something unless you have a positive feeling about it.

When a war starts, nobody knows how many people will be killed or what we will lose forever. Both sides think they will win, but no one can predict what will happen. Even when one side wins, things can get worse rather than better. There is no winning in wars or in earthquakes.

Name _____ Date _____

Directions: In the table below, write the scores you give the expository essay for its execution of the six writing traits. (The highest score is 5; the lowest is 1.) Then write some comments that explain the scores you gave. Use specific examples from the text to support your evaluations.

Expository Essay: Six Trait Scores	
Trait	**Score**
Ideas and Content	
Organization	
Voice	
Word Choice	
Sentence Fluency	
Conventions	
Overall Comments:	

EVALUATING A PERSUASIVE ESSAY USING THE SIX WRITING TRAITS

Directions: A student responded to the persuasive prompt below. Read the student's essay and the completed evaluation on the next page. Then answer the questions that follow.

next page

Persuasive Prompt *Imagine that a local builder found an ancient campsite while clearing land to build a badly needed school. Should the builder be allowed to proceed, or should building stop while archaeologists study the site? Local schools are overcrowded, and archaeologists estimate that it could take as long as a year to complete their study. Write an essay for your school newspaper in which you state your position on this issue and support it with convincing reasons and details.*

If construction of a new school for our city is suspended for a year, as archaeologists want, some classes in our old school will have fifty or more students next year. I know it is important to make discoveries at the ancient campsite, but I think a year is too long to wait to start building a new school. I think we should give the archaeologists a shorter time to dig so we don't spend another whole year crowded into an old building and trailers. I believe that technology can help both projects get done faster and that people on both sides want the best for history and for children.

Technology can help in two ways. I think the archaeologists should get one of those machines that lets them see objects underground. If they see anything out of the ordinary, they should start digging immediately. If they find nothing in a period of five months, we should start to build the foundation for our new school. During the time when the archaeologists are looking at the site, the new school can be designed, and we can use computer programs to plan and figure out the most efficient way to do the job. That way, as soon as the archaeologists finish, we can be ready to start work right away and finish the school more quickly.

If I were an archaeologist, of course I would want

Notes

to dig up whatever treasure is underground. They might learn more about early humans or maybe even find something that can confirm the way dinosaurs died, and then they would want to keep digging. Still, if I were an archaeologist, I would probably want the best for the children. After all, archaeologists spent a lot of time in school. They know it's important. They might even have kids, too. The archaeologists should try to finish their project as soon as they can so that the school will be ready by the next school year. If I were an archaeologist, I would not want my work to force kids to stay crowded in an old school.

On the other hand, if I were an administrator, obviously I would want to build the school. However, I would probably be interested in finding out what was at the site, too. If there were fossils or artifacts to be found, I would have the archaeologists start digging. Their discoveries might give us further things to study in our new school, and our school would be recognized as the place where an important discovery was made. Finding fossils at our new school will give us an advantage, but stopping construction for a whole year would mean the old school will still be crowded and put the students at a disadvantage.

The best solution to this problem is to limit the delay caused by digging at the site. The archaeologists and builders should use technology to speed up the process so that construction of the new school can begin in time for the school to be ready for the next school year. We deserve to go to a new school that is not overcrowded.

One Reader's Evaluation

A reader used the rubrics on pages 25–39 to evaluate the persuasive essay on pages 47–48. Below are her scores and comments.

Persuasive Essay: Six Trait Scores	
Trait	**Score**
Ideas and Content: The writer identifies a clear position and considers multiple perspectives, although the ideas sometimes lack specificity.	4
Organization: Organization fits the writer's purpose, and ideas progress logically.	5
Voice: The writer demonstrates a keen involvement with the topic, but uses a fair and calm voice as he or she discusses possible concerns from opposing viewpoints.	4
Word Choice: Word choice is correct and adequate to communicate the writer's ideas.	3
Sentence Fluency: Sentences vary in length and structure and clearly communicate the writer's message.	5
Conventions: The writer demonstrates control over the conventions of written language; paragraphing, grammar, punctuation, capitalization, and spelling are generally correct.	5
Overall Comments:	
Overall I thought the paper was balanced, thoughtful, and interested in the topic. I could tell the writer cared deeply about both building a new school and making historical discoveries.	

What's the Score? Sometimes a trait in a paper may deserve a score of a 4 or a 2. The rubrics don't show those scores, though. Use your judgment. If you think that a paper's organization is not quite a 5 but definitely better than a 3, you can always give a score of 4.

Name _____ Date _____

Your Turn

Now answer the questions below. Use the rubrics on pages 25–39 to figure out how you would score the preceding persuasive essay (pages 47–48). How do your responses compare to the scores given by the reader on the previous page?

1. I do/ do not agree with the evaluator's score on the writer's ideas and content because

   _____

   _____

2. I do/ do not agree with the evaluator's score on the writer's organization because

   _____

   _____

3. I do/ do not agree with the evaluator's score on the writer's voice because

   _____

   _____

4. I do/ do not agree with the evaluator's score on the writer's word choice because

   _____

   _____

5. I do/ do not agree with the evaluator's score on the writer's sentence fluency because

   _____

   _____

6. I do/ do not agree with the evaluator's score on the writer's conventions because

   _____

   _____

7. If you were to give the essay different scores from the ones on page 49, what would they be?

   _____

   _____

PRACTICE EVALUATING A PERSUASIVE ESSAY

Persuasive Essay: Read the prompt and the persuasive essay below. Then review the six traits rubrics on pages 25–39. Use the blank evaluation form that follows to score the writer's work.

Persuasive Prompt *Are school uniforms a restriction on individual freedom? Do uniforms help maintain discipline and reduce the pressure to wear the "right" clothes? Write a well-organized paper in which you state and give reasons for your opinion on this issue.*

Are school uniforms a restriction on individual freedom? Do uniforms help to maintain discipline and reduce the pressure to wear the "right" clothes?

Some say yes, some say no. Individual freedom is defined as the freedom that an individual has. Also discipline is defined as the rules a person must obey or be punished. "Right" clothes is defined as what everybody says is cool. You have to wear the "right" clothes—certain types or brands of shirts, pants, and shoes—to school to be cool. Some kids don't have the "right" clothes and don't fit in. Maybe they would like to wear uniforms. Not everybody likes uniforms, though. Certainly not me.

If a person is acting up in the hall and showing off, it doesn't have anything to do with what clothes the person is wearing. Wearing a uniform won't change someone's behavior. It won't make you be a good student or a trouble maker. Uniforms just make everyone look the same. Why would I want to look like everyone else? I like having style. I don't want my freedom taken away.

At our school an assist. principle tells the girls all the time there have too short skirts and calls their parents. They have to change clothes or go home. What a waste of time! They just sit around in the office waiting for some one to bring them different clothes or pick them up. How does that help them learn anything? School is about learning.

Notes

One friend tole me she has school uniforms at her school. She think they are terrible. That school won't let them do anything to show how cool they are. Not even to their hair. She says when school is out, she changes clothes super fast. She wants to throw her uniform in the trash. She hates wearing black and blue again. At her school the uniforms are not even the school colors, which are gold and purple. Their team is called the Bruins and the football team has a cool uniform. Not like my friend who has a terrible uniform because they make her wear it.

We need our freedom because we will learn to drive soon and be in high school. With or without uniforms we need freedom. We need to take care of making our own decisions about stuff like clothes. We need to be able to show how cool we are. But, some say there's too much pressure to be cool and wear the "right" clothes. I can see that too, so what do you think?

In conclusion, it may be a restriction of individual rights and freedoms. Or a disciple maintainer, or to avoid the peer pressure. What is right for you, you do.

Name _____   Date _____

Directions: In the table below, write the scores you give the persuasive essay for its execution of the six writing traits. (The highest score is 5; the lowest is 1.) Then write some comments that explain the scores you gave. Use specific examples from the text to support your evaluations.

Persuasive Essay: Six Trait Scores	
Trait	**Score**
Ideas and Content	
Organization	
Voice	
Word Choice	
Sentence Fluency	
Conventions	
Overall Comments:	

EVALUATING A NARRATIVE ESSAY USING THE SIX WRITING TRAITS

Directions: A student responded to the narrative prompt below. Read the student's essay and the completed evaluation on the next page. Then answer the questions that follow.

Narrative Prompt *Think of an important event or incident in your life. What lesson did you learn? Write a well-developed personal narrative that describes the experience and reveals why it was important to you.*

Sometimes my imagination takes off too quickly. One day my parents, my sister Elena, and I were driving to Virginia for a long weekend. I was looking at a brochure for the place we were going to stay. "Hey, Mom," I said, "they have hot-air balloon rides." Dad asked whether we would like to try it. Without hesitating, I said, "Sure." Mom offered to call for reservations. "Goody," squealed Elena.

I imagined the balloon ride. What had I been thinking? I had agreed to go up in a little basket attached to a balloon. "There is no way of steering the vehicle," the brochure explained, "so it just goes with the wind." Panic set in. I comforted myself with the thought that Mom probably couldn't get reservations so late.

When we got to the hotel, Mom called about the balloon ride. Elena stood beside her, looking eager. I was thinking, "Please say you don't have room for us." Mom got off the phone and announced cheerfully, "We meet the balloonist at 6:30 a.m." Elena was thrilled. I was imagining what my friends would say when they heard how I had drifted away into the pillowy clouds or worse, slammed into a building.

Notes

I tossed and turned all night and dreamed of crash landings in the desert. Never mind that there are no deserts in Virginia. Finally, morning came. My last hope was that it would rain, but a peek out the window took away that hope. Soon people would be rescuing me from a tree.

We waited outside. My fears quadrupled when I saw the balloonist drive up. The basket on the back of the truck couldn't possibly hold all of us. We drove to a field as the sun popped over the horizon. The team prepared the balloon. Everyone else in my family was fascinated. I felt sick. My dad noticed I was quiet, and asked what was wrong. "I'm scared," I replied. He said, "It can be scary to do something new, but just imagine what the view will be like." Then he squeezed my hand, and I felt better. Finally, we climbed into the tiny basket with the balloon pilot. Once we were settled, the team let go of the ropes. In no time, we were softly gliding upward over the velvety, rolling hills. "Hey, this is great!" I yelled. I had to laugh when I realized how much time I had wasted worrying. Sometimes I need to listen to my imagination.

One Reader's Evaluation

A reader used the rubrics on pages 25–39 to evaluate the narrative essay on pages 54–55. Below are her scores and comments.

Narrative Essay: Six Trait Scores	
Trait	**Score**
Ideas and Content: A clear idea—overcoming fear—governs the narrative. The reader receives a clear idea of the character of the narrator and his or her sister. Appropriate details about the parents are required for plot development. The writer obviously learned a lesson and shares it with the readers.	5
Organization: The organizational structure effectively incorporates internal dialogue and suspense to move the plot along, and the narrative builds to an effective resolution that suggests a lesson about life.	5
Voice: The writer's voice is clear and engaging and demonstrates a thoughtful approach to the writing task.	5
Word Choice: Word choice is specific and effective.	5
Sentence Fluency: The narrative uses a variety of sentence types and structures. The sentences flow nicely and have a nice pace, speeding up or slowing down the action as appropriate.	5
Conventions: The writer demonstrates a strong command of the conventions of the English language.	5
Overall Comments:	
Overall I thought the paper was insightful, clear, and fun to read. I could tell the writer understood how the experience affected his or her life.	

A Closer Look. Think about the writer's purpose when you give scores for organization. For example, the purpose of a narrative is to tell a story. Usually the events should be organized in the order that they occur. If they are out of order or hard to follow, you need to give a lower score for organization.

Name _____ Date _____

Your Turn

Now answer the questions below. Use the rubrics on pages 25–39 to figure out how you would score the preceding narrative essay (pages 54–55). How do your responses compare to the scores given by the reader on the previous page?

1. I do/ do not agree with the evaluator's score on the writer's ideas and content because

_____

_____

2. I do/ do not agree with the evaluator's score on the writer's organization because

_____

_____

3. I do/ do not agree with the evaluator's score on the writer's voice because

_____

_____

4. I do/ do not agree with the evaluator's score on the writer's word choice because

_____

_____

5. I do/ do not agree with the evaluator's score on the writer's sentence fluency because

_____

_____

6. I do/ do not agree with the evaluator's score on the writer's conventions because

_____

_____

7. If you were to give the essay different scores from the ones on page 56, what would they be?

_____

_____

PRACTICE EVALUATING A NARRATIVE ESSAY

Narrative Essay: Read the prompt and the narrative essay below. Then review the six traits rubrics on pages 25–39 and fill in the blank evaluation form that follows.

Narrative Prompt

Think of an important event or incident that happened to you recently. What lesson did you learn? Write a well-developed personal narrative that describes the experience and reveals why it was important to you.

The ringing phone jarred me awake. "Hello," I answered somewhat sternly, wondering who would dare to call me so early on Saturday morning.

"Get up, Maria. We're going to an air show today. Be ready in half an hour."

Before I could even object, Uncle Raul hung up. It's true; Uncle Raul usually took me to interesting events, but an air show? At that moment, sleeping late seemed much more appealing.

Still, I got dressed, ate breakfast, and greeted my uncle thirty minutes later. "This had better be a good show," I warned.

As he drove to the field, he described the Thunderbirds, an elite squadron of Air Force pilots. I listened in silence, too sleepy and grumpy to be excited. When we arrived, I was surprised to see a large number of people standing at the edge of a huge airfield. We finally found a place to stand in the growing crowd.

Six gigantic F-16 jets sat on the runway. The gleaming white bodies of the fighter planes threw off a glare in the hot sun, and I shielded my eyes with my hand. The wings, nose, and tail of each jet were painted with three stripes. The first was red, the next white, and the last one a blue so dark that it looked like the night sky. Over each right wing were the letters USAF.

Notes

Six Traits for Writing Success, Middle School

Just then, an announcement crackled over a loudspeaker. The show was beginning. Six pilots dressed in bright red jumpsuits marched briskly onto the airfield. They climbed into the cockpits and pulled on their shiny helmets. A loud BOOM shook the crowd as the pilots started the jet engines. The pilots then turned to the crowd, gave a thumbs-up sign, and the six jets roared off into the air.

The squadron turned and headed back over the airfield in a diamond formation. Streams of white smoke trailed behind them in the brilliant blue sky. The jets flew so close together that they looked as though their wings were actually touching. They made another pass over us, doing flips and rolls and dives. The announcer called out the names of the maneuvers: "Five Card Loop, Wing Rock-and-Roll, Cuban Eight." Several times I found myself gasping, thinking the jets were about to crash.

Back and forth, up and down, the F-16s roared overhead. Without our noticing it, one jet peeled off from the others. Suddenly it appeared out of nowhere, roaring over our heads. The ground shook. It sounded like a bomb exploding right behind us. We screamed and laughed in relief as the single jet joined the others.

Too soon, the show was over. The Thunderbirds landed, taxied down the runway, and parked. The crowd cheered wildly as the pilots approached, shaking hands, saluting, and signing autographs. I applauded and cheered along with everyone else.

Uncle Raul looked over at me and said, "Well, was this worth getting up for?" I smiled sheepishly. Once again, he gave me an experience I would never forget. Never again would I doubt him.

Notes

Name _____ Date _____

Directions: In the table below, write the scores you give the narrative essay for its execution of the six writing traits. (The highest score is 5; the lowest is 1.) Then write some comments that explain the scores you gave. Use specific examples from the text to support your evaluations.

Narrative Essay: Six Trait Scores	
Trait	**Score**
Ideas and Content	
Organization	
Voice	
Word Choice	
Sentence Fluency	
Conventions	
Overall Comments:	

PART THREE

Using the Six Traits to Write

HOW TO READ A WRITING PROMPT

A prompt is a writing assignment. Most prompts provide you with a topic for writing and identify the audience for which you should write. The formats of writing prompts will vary. Prompts may ask questions, tell you to respond to a quotation, or set up a hypothetical situation.

Here is an example of a persuasive writing prompt.

> *Your state is considering new policy that would require a young person to have a high school diploma before he or she can apply for a driver's license. What do you think? Write a letter to the editor of your local newspaper stating your opinion and supporting it with convincing reasons.*

Steps for Reading and Analyzing a Prompt

STEP 1 **Read the prompt carefully to identify your task or purpose for writing.** Make sure you understand what you are being asked to write about. Think about how you will address the topic. Does the prompt tell you to write an essay or another form of writing (like a letter)?

STEP 2 **Determine your audience.** Think about who will be reading your essay. If your audience is not stated directly, assume that it is the general adult population.

STEP 3 **Decide on your topic.** What is the key idea or opinion that the prompt wants you to discuss? Do you need to choose your own specific topic to fit a general question?

STEP 4 **Look for cue words.** Not every prompt will have a label telling what kind of writing is expected. Look for words that indicate your task or purpose. (See the chart below.)

Type of Prompt	Cue Words	Task or Purpose
Expository	*explain what, how,* or *why*	Give facts, ideas, or other kinds of information on a topic or explain how to do something.
Persuasive	*convince, persuade,* or *defend*	Take a point of view on an issue and provide reasons and evidence that support your opinion.
Narrative	*tell, retell, recall,* or *remember*	Tell about or recall a meaningful event. Include interesting and specific details, dialogue, and characters to express your ideas.

READING AND ANALYZING PROMPTS

Directions: Read each of the prompts below. Then identify the topic, purpose, and audience of each prompt. Circle cue words that help you determine the purpose—expository, persuasive, or narrative.

Prompt 1 Think of something you have done that you are proud of. Write a well-developed personal essay in which you recall the situation and describe why it makes you proud. Select an even that you feel comfortable sharing with readers.

Topic: _____

Purpose: _____

Audience: _____

Prompt 2 After a number of incidents of illegal activity in your area, local politicians are considering instituting a 9 p.m. curfew for all teenagers. Take a stand on the issue and write a letter to the editor of your local newspaper defending your position on the curfew. Be sure to provide reasons to support your opinion.

Topic: _____

Purpose: _____

Audience: _____

Prompt 3 The concept of honor has been an important one in all the cultures of the world. As a result, many people have thought and written about honor, both the idea and the act of honoring. Read the following questions about honor. Then write an essay for your school newspaper explaining the meaning of honor, to be published on Memorial Day or Veteran's Day.

"Any person of honor chooses rather than to lose his honor than to lose his conscience."
Michel de Montaigne

"Honor to the Soldier, and Sailor everywhere, who bravely bears his country's cause. Honor also to the citizen who cares for his brother in the field, and servers, as best he can, the same cause..." *Abraham Lincoln*

Topic: _____

Purpose: _____

Audience: _____

WRITING WORKSHOP 1: USING THE SIX TRAITS TO WRITE EXPOSITORY TEXT

The purpose of an expository, or informative, text is to inform. The main intent is for you to present clear information. Expository writing is used to share knowledge and to convey messages, instructions, and ideas.

(PREWRITING)   The prewriting stage is where you do the work of identifying your purpose and audience, deciding what to write about, and planning. *Three of the six traits will help you here.*

💭 IDEAS AND CONTENT

• *Explore ideas and choose a topic.*

Ask questions about subjects that interest you. Try finding a topic by brainstorming. Take about five minutes to write down every question or idea that pops into your head. Don't judge yourself! After your time is up, reread your questions or ideas. Choose the question or idea that you want to develop in your paper. (See the worksheet on page 91.)

Quick Tip   In a test situation, a writing prompt will usually give you a specific topic to write about, but you will still need to gather ideas, develop a main idea, and plan.

• *Gather ideas and details to develop the topic.*

Look at good, reliable sources of information, such as books, magazines, encyclopedias, trusted websites, and experts in your community. Take notes about your topic. You can use these notes later to provide logical support for your ideas. Write down interesting facts, examples, statistics, and expert opinions.

• *Think about your audience and your purpose for writing.*

Ask "Who am I writing for?" "What do my readers need to know?" "What will they find interesting?" Remember that your purpose is to inform.

ORGANIZATION

• *Develop a thesis or controlling idea.*

Narrow your topic so that it is not too big. For example, the topic of your three favorite sports is too big. An explanation of the field-goal kick is too narrow. You need something in between, such as how the way football is played has changed over the last ten years.

• *Organize the ideas and details into a coherent structure.*

Try using order of importance. Start with your least important idea and save the most important idea for last. That way, the reader will remember it better. Use a graphic organizer like the one below to organize your ideas in order of importance. (See the worksheet on page 99.)

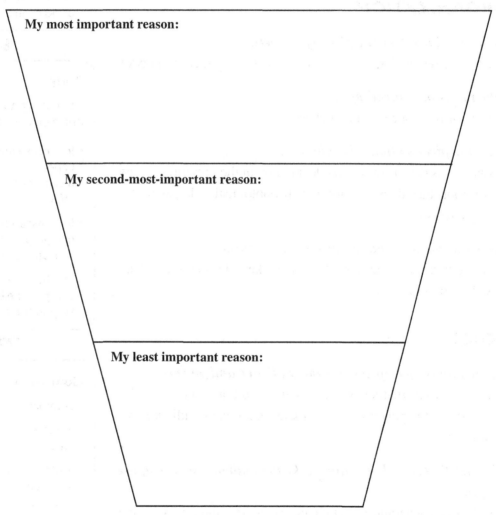

My most important reason:

My second-most-important reason:

My least important reason:

 VOICE

• *Think about your audience. What voice should you use?*

Your tone (friendly, calm, stern, neutral) should match your purpose and your topic. A paper about how to make a clown costume can have a friendly, informal voice. A paper about the causes and effects of air pollution needs to be formal and serious. (For help with voice, see page 10.)

WRITING Writing is the stage where you express your main ideas clearly, support those ideas, and follow a plan of organization, adjusting the plan as needed to make meaning clear. *Five of the six traits will help you here.*

IDEAS AND CONTENT

• *Develop paragraphs that support your main idea.*
Each paragraph should focus on one aspect of the topic. Be sure to provide definitions and background information about your topic. Elaborate on your ideas by including specific examples and details.

ORGANIZATION

• *Decide how to introduce the piece effectively.*
Try to grab your readers' attention with an interesting fact or anecdote.

• *State the thesis or controlling idea.*
Make sure your main idea is stated clearly.

• *Organize the piece so that it is coherent.*
As you write, consider the order you decided on in the prewriting stage. If order of importance doesn't work, try chronological order, spatial order, or logical order.

• *Conclude the paper so that it has a sense of closure.*
Don't leave your readers hanging. Review the key ideas and then leave readers with a final thought.

VOICE

• *Use a tone that is appropriate for the audience and purpose.*
Use a consistent voice that keeps readers engaged but is serious and formal enough for the purpose of your essay. Keep your audience in mind as you write.

• *Include cues that signal tone and make the audience aware of the paper's purpose.*
For example, in a cause-and-effect paper, use words and phrases such as *cause, effect, affect, because, as a result, in the end, so,* and *resulting in.*

Introduction
• Attention-grabbing beginning
• Main idea statement
• Definitions and/or background information

Body
Each paragraph focuses on one aspect of the topic.

• In a cause and effect paper, each paragraph discusses a cause or effect.

• In a research paper, each paragraph addresses one subtopic or key idea.

• In a how-to paper, each paragraph explains one step in the process.

Conclusion
• Summary of ideas
• Restatement of main idea
• Additional insight into the topic

WORD CHOICE

• *As you write, use language that effectively conveys your ideas.*

Choose words that you understand and that communicate your meaning exactly. If you use unfamiliar vocabulary or jargon, make sure you define the terms and use them properly.

• *Use formal, but natural sounding language.*

Most expository papers have a serious and formal voice. Choose words that match the voice of your paper but still let your voice shine through. An expository paper should be interesting even though the voice is formal. Avoid clichés and idioms.

 SENTENCE FLUENCY

• *Look at how your sentences flow and connect ideas.*

Include effective transitions between sentences and paragraphs that show the connections between ideas. Vary your sentence constructions, too. Use a mixture of long and short sentences and include sentences that start with phrases or clauses.

Ways to Vary Sentence Structure
Begin a Sentence with a Phrase
ORIGINAL: The city council will hold its next meeting in June.
VARIATION: In June, the city council will hold its next meeting.
Begin a Sentence with a Clause
ORIGINAL: The fire damaged the community center, and it had to be rebuilt.
VARIATION: Because the fire damaged the community center, it had to be rebuilt.
Combining Sentences by Using *And*, *But*, or *Or*
ORIGINAL: Many nations use the metric system. The United States uses its own system of measurement.
COMBINED: Many nations use the metric system, **but** the United States uses its own system of measurement.
Combining by Using a Subordinate Clause
ORIGINAL: Elizabeth Cady Stanton was a civil rights activist. She fought to win women the right to vote in federal elections.
COMBINED: Elizabeth Cady Stanton was a civil rights activist **who** fought to win women the right to vote in federal elections.

The revising and evaluating stage may be the most important in the process of writing an expository paper. It is where you figure out if your ideas, organization, and style are working and if you are communicating your ideas clearly. *Five of the six traits will help you here.*

💭 IDEAS AND CONTENT

• *Evaluate and revise the ideas and content of the paper.*

Do all your ideas and details "fit" the paper and support your main idea? Did you provide definitions and background information to help readers understand your writing? Have you included enough details and examples to support your ideas? Use the Guidelines for Self-Evaluation on page 70. They will help you decide if you need to edit or revise any of your ideas and content.

Quick Tip **Edit or Revise?** Many people use the words *edit* and *revise* interchangeably. Dictionaries define *edit* as "to revise and make a text ready for publication." They define *revise* as "to correct and improve a text." Follow your teacher's guidance here.

✚ ORGANIZATION

• *Evaluate and revise the organization of the paper.*

Have you placed your ideas in a way that makes sense to the reader and suits the topic? Did you include a concluding statement at the end of the papert? Use the Guidelines for Self-Evaluation on page 70. They will help you decide if you need to change your organizational structure.

🔊 VOICE

• *Refine the style of the paper so that it suits the audience and purpose and conveys the appropriate voice.*

Your voice lets readers know what you think about your topic and your audience. Are you friendly or formal, concerned or indifferent? Let readers know through your tone and style. (See page 10 in this book for help with voice.)

Passive voice expresses an action done to the subject. Active voice expresses an action done by the subject.

Use active voice as much as possible. It makes your writing clearer and more direct. To identify passive voice, look for forms of *be* used as helping verbs.

Passive Voice	Active Voice
The tree was knocked over by the wind.	The wind knocked over the tree.
The play was performed by the eighth graders.	The eighth graders performed the play.
Mistakes were made by the defensive team.	The defensive team made mistakes.
The prize is won by the student with the highest grade.	The student with the highest grade wins the prize.

WORD CHOICE

• *Evaluate and revise the words you use.*

Your choice of words should reflect your attitude toward your subject and audience. Think about the connotations of the words you use in your writing. (See pages 11–12 for help with word choice.)

SENTENCE FLUENCY

• *Evaluate and revise the way you connect ideas in your sentences and paragraphs.*

You may think the connections between your ideas are obvious, but you know your material better than the reader does. Use transitional words and phrases to show those connections. Also, make sure some of your sentences start with phrases or clauses, to make your writing more interesting. (Also, see pages 13–14 for help with sentence fluency.)

Guidelines for Self-Evaluation

Evaluation Questions	Tip	Editing/Revision Techniques
IDEAS AND CONTENT 1. Does the introduction include a clear main idea statement? Does the paper have a conclusion that summarizes the main points and closes with an interesting observation?	**Underline** the main idea. Ask whether it identifies a clear and interesting idea. **Draw a box** around the conclusion. Ask if it accurately reflects the content of your paper and includes an interesting observation.	**Add** a clear statement of the main idea if one is missing. If the conclusion does not summarize your main points, **add** a summary. If it does not have an interesting observation, **add** one.
ORGANIZATION 2. Does each paragraph discuss or focus on one idea? Does the support flow logically from one idea to the next?	Put a **check** by each idea in a paragraph. Put an **asterisk** next to each supporting detail.	**Rearrange** the ideas and support so that each paragraph contains one idea and its supporting evidence.
VOICE 3. Is the tone of the paper appropriate for the audience?	In the margins, **write** an adjective that describes the tone of voice in each paragraph.	If the tone changes abruptly or does not match the content or the audience, **adjust** word choice and phrasing to make it more appropriate.
WORD CHOICE 4. Do you use words that help readers understand your ideas? Do you use helpful cue words or phrases? Do your words add life to your writing?	**Circle** all the cue words or phrases in a paragraph. **Draw boxes** around words or phrases that add "flavor" to your writing.	If a paragraph has no circled words, reread it and see where you can **add** cue words or phrases. If no words are boxed, consult a thesaurus to find synonyms that have more flavor.
SENTENCE FLUENCY 5. Do transitions help flow ideas together coherently?	**Mark** transitional words or phrases with **stars**.	**Add** transitional words or phrases if needed.

Publishing is the stage in the writing process where you make your paper ready for your actual readers. *As you prepare your paper for publication, consider four of the six traits.*

IDEAS AND CONTENT

• *Reflect on your completed paper.*

Consider how you might approach a similar writing assignment next time. Ask yourself the following questions:

• How well did I achieve the purpose of sharing information with my audience?

• Which part of my final draft was most effective? Which was the least effective?

• The part of writing an informative paper that I liked most/least was….

◀ VOICE

• *Publish your paper for its intended audience.*

Think about the tone and attitude you convey in your paper. Ask yourself if the voice you used really suited both your topic and your audience.

SENTENCE FLUENCY

• *Evaluate and revise the way you connect ideas in your sentences and paragraphs.*

You may think the connections between your ideas are obvious, but you know your material better than the reader does. Use transitional words and phrases to show those connections. Also, make sure some of your sentences start with phrases or clauses, to make your writing more interesting. (Also, see pages 13–14 for help with sentence fluency.)

◣ CONVENTIONS

• *Proofread and edit the paper to catch and correct errors in paragraphing, spelling, capitalization, punctuation, and grammar.*

Take care not to let any distracting errors slip into your published paper. Give your paper a final proofread using the convention errors checklist on pages 15–16.

Expository Writing Prompts for Practice

Remember, **expository, or informative, writing prompts will ask you to explain something**. Use the writing process and the six traits to prepare responses to these prompts. Write your responses on your own paper. Use the self-evaluation rubrics on pages 126–132 to evaluate your responses.

Practice Prompts

Prompt 1 Most people have a favorite season of the year. Think about which season you like best. Then explain in an essay why this season is your favorite. Be sure to use sensory details to support your response.

Prompt 2 Some teachers grade students on class participation. Write an essay in which you explain both what is good and what is bad about grading for class participation. Be sure to explain each point fully and to be balanced in your discussion.

Prompt 3 Think of something you have succeeded in doing—an accomplishment, a goal you met, or a dream you realized. Then explain how you reached your success. Describe each step in the process, including setbacks and lucky breaks. Finally, tell readers what you learned from the experience.

Prompt 4 Think about the qualities of a successful person—a professional athlete, a world-class musician, a fine writer, or a scientist who makes a world-changing discovery. What do you think causes or inspires people to be great? In an essay, talk about the causes or effects of greatness. The effects may be positive, negative, or both. Use examples from real life, books, movies, and television.

Prompt 5 The United States has been described as a "great melting pot" in which people of all backgrounds come together and are blended into a single, democratic society. Write an essay in which you explain how American society is or is not like a melting pot today. You may use examples from real life as well as from books, movies, or television shows.

Prompt 6 In his second inaugural address in 1937, President Franklin D. Roosevelt addressed a nation that was still experiencing widespread economic depression. He said, "The test of our progress is not whether we add more to the abundance of those who have much; it is whether we provide enough for those who have too little." Write an essay that explains what Roosevelt meant in this quotation. You may use examples from real life, books, movies, or television.

WRITING WORKSHOP 11: USING THE SIX TRAITS TO WRITE PERSUASIVE TEXT

Remember that your purpose is to persuade. The main intent is for you to state a clear opinion and support it with convincing evidence. Persuasive writing is used to share opinions and to influence readers' thoughts, opinions, feelings, and actions.

(PREWRITING) Prewriting is the stage in which you choose an interesting issue and determine your opinion. *Three of the six traits will help you here.*

💭 IDEAS AND CONTENT

• *Explore ideas and choose an issue.*

Look around you. Remember that an issue is a subject about which people disagree. Read newspapers and talk to family and friends.

When you think you have found a good issue, ask yourself these questions:
• Is the issue debatable? Will people disagree about it?
• Do I have strong feelings about the issue?
• Would other people have strong feelings?

> **Quick Tip** In a test situation, a persuasive writing prompt may provide you with an issue and even an opinion to argue. You may not care deeply about the issue, but you must write persuasively. Use your brains, not your heart. Think of as much evidence as you can and present it in a logical way.

• *State your opinion.*

An opinion statement—which will be your thesis statement or main idea—is a statement that tells both the issue and your point of view. It lets readers know where you stand.

• *Think about your audience.*

Ask "What type of people will read my paper?" "How do they probably feel about the issue?" "What objections might they have to my ideas?"

• *Evaluate and support reasons.*

Do some research. Make sure that there are good reasons and solid evidence to support your opinion. Reasons tell why you have a particular point of view. Evidence includes facts, statistics, examples, anecdotes, and expert opinions. Evidence backs up your claim and makes it credible or believable.

ORGANIZATION

• *Organize the ideas and details logically.*

Effective persuasive writing is usually organized in a logical way. Think of at least three reasons to support your opinion. Then support each reason with evidence. Group your ideas logically. Use a graphic organizer, like the one below, to help you organize your ideas. (See the worksheet on page 98.)

 VOICE

• *Think about the tone you should use.*

Writers who want to appeal to their readers' sense of reason should use a voice that is serious, formal, and polite. (For help with voice, see page 10.)

WRITING The writing stage is where you put your ideas down on paper. *Five of the six traits will help you with writing your persuasive paper.*

IDEAS AND CONTENT

• *Develop sentences and paragraphs that identify your opinion and support it with persuasive evidence.*

Each sentence and paragraph should focus on one complete thought or idea. Make sure you have enough to talk about. Each reason should have at least one piece of evidence to support it.

ORGANIZATION

• *Grab readers' attention by appealing to their self-interest.*

First, identify the issue in an interesting way. Then tell readers how the issue affects them every day.

• *State your opinion up front.*

Tell your readers exactly what you think about the issue in the introduction. A clear statement of your position will help readers prepare for your arguments and make their way through the next paragraphs.

• *Use logical appeal.*

Order of importance works best in persuasive papers. Dedicate at least one paragraph to each of your reasons. Support the reasons with evidence. Elaborate on the evidence so that readers understand exactly what you mean.

• *Conclude the paper with a call to action.*

Restate your opinion and your reasons. Then close with a call to action—tell readers what you want them to do or think. Make sure your call to action identifies a specific action and not just a general idea about the issue.

VOICE

• *Use your voice to convey the importance of the issue.*

Make sure your voice reflects the seriousness of the topic. Also, even if your readers disagree with your opinion, they deserve your respect. Use a voice that conveys respect and intelligence. Consider using the first-person point of view.

Introduction
• Attention-grabbing beginning
• Opinion statement

Body
Each paragraph focuses on one aspect of the topic.
• Reason #1
• Evidence and elaboration
• Reason #2
• Evidence and elaboration and so on

Conclusion
• Restatement of opinion
• Summary of reasons
• Call to action or closing statement

WORD CHOICE

• *As you write, use language that effectively conveys your ideas.*
Choose words that clearly and accurately describe the issue. If you must use jargon or technical terms, define the terms in ways that your target audience will understand.

• *Avoid loaded language.*
Be careful not to slip into using a lot of loaded language, words with strong connotations that provoke a strong reaction. Persuasive writing should be based primarily on logical support and factual evidence, not on emotional appeals. If you use too much loaded language, the audience may think you are too biased and not take your argument seriously.

 SENTENCE FLUENCY

• *Make clear transitions between ideas.*
You want your readers to follow your argument. Use sentences that are clear and succinct. Also, be sure to use clear transitional words and phrases to help readers understand how your details and evidence support your argument or position. (See the worksheet on page 111.)

Chronological Order	*after, at last, at once, before, eventually, finally, first, later, meanwhile, next, soon, then, when, while*
Cause and Effect	*as a result, because, consequently, for, for this reason, since, so, so that, therefore*
Spatial Order	*above, across, among, around, before, behind, below, beneath, by, down, here, in, inside, into, near, next to, over, there, under, up*
Order of Importance	*first, last, mainly, more important, then, to begin with*
Comparison	*also, and, another, just as, like, likewise, moreover, similarly, too*
Contrast	*although, but, however, in spite of, instead, nevertheless, on the other hand, otherwise, still, yet*

The revising and evaluating stage is where you figure out if your ideas, organization, and style are working and if you are communicating your ideas clearly. *Five of the six traits will help you here.*

IDEAS AND CONTENT

• *Evaluate and revise your opinion and evidence.*
Is your opinion clearly stated? Is it adequately supported by reasons and evidence? Use the Guidelines for Self-Evaluation on page 78 to determine if you need to revise your ideas and content.

ORGANIZATION

• *Evaluate and revise the organization of the paper.*
Have you organized your argument in a way that makes sense to the reader and suits the issue? Use the Guidelines for Self-Evaluation to evaluate your organizational structure.

VOICE

• *Refine your style to convey the appropriate voice.*
Your voice lets readers know what you think about your topic and your audience. Are you friendly or formal, concerned or indifferent? Let readers know through your tone and style. (See page 10.)

> **Quick Tip** *Avoid Emotional Appeal*
> Emotional appeal is another persuasive tactic. It involves using language and ideas that appeal to readers' feelings rather than to their intellect. It is a powerful technique but can easily backfire. It relies on the writer's voice more than on evidence. In testing situations, it is best to stick with logical appeal.

WORD CHOICE

• *Evaluate and revise the words you use.*
Your choice of words should reflect your attitude toward the issue and your audience. As you revise, make sure that you have not used loaded language. Make sure you know the connotations of the words you use. (See pages 11–12.)

SENTENCE FLUENCY

• *Evaluate and revise the way you connect ideas in your sentences and paragraphs.*
Are your transitional words and phrases clear? Did you begin some sentences with phrases and clauses for variety? (See pages 13–14.)

Guidelines for Self-Evaluation

Evaluation Questions	Tip	Editing/Revision Techniques
◻ IDEAS AND CONTENT 1. Does the introduction include a clear main idea statement? Does the paper have a conclusion that summarizes the main points and closes with an interesting observation?	**Underline** the opinion. Ask whether it expresses a point of view. **Draw** a box around the conclusion. Make sure it restates the opinion and includes a call to action.	**Add** a clear opinion if one is missing. If the conclusion does not summarize your reasons, **add** a summary. If it does not have an call to action, **add** one.
✿ ORGANIZATION 2. Do the paragraphs progress in order of importance? Does the writer give reasons to support the opinion? Are the reasons supported by evidence?	**Number** the paragraphs in order of importance. **Put a star** next to each reason and **highlight** the evidence for each reason.	**Rearrange** the order of paragraphs, if necessary. **Add** a reason, or **add** a fact, statistic, anecdote, example, or expert opinion to support a reason, if necessary.
◣ VOICE 3. Is the tone of the paper appropriate for the audience?	In the margins, **write** an adjective that describes the tone of voice in each paragraph.	If the tone changes abruptly or does not match the content or the audience, **adjust** the language to make it more appropriate.
▦ WORD CHOICE 4. Do you use opinion words that help readers understand your point of view? Do your words add spice to your writing?	**Circle** all the opinion words or phrases in a paragraph. **Draw boxes** around words or phrases that you think add "flavor" to your writing.	If a paragraph has no circled words, reread it and see where you can **add** opinion words or phrases. If no words are boxed, **consult** a thesaurus to find synonyms that have more flavor.
≋ SENTENCE FLUENCY 5. Do transitions help flow ideas together logically and coherently?	**Mark** transitional words or phrases **with stars**.	**Add** transitional words or phrases if needed.

PUBLISHING Publishing is the stage in the writing process where you make your paper ready for your actual readers. *As you prepare your paper for publication, consider four of the six traits.*

IDEAS AND CONTENT

• *Reflect on your completed paper.*

Consider how you might approach a similar writing assignment next time. Ask yourself the following questions:

• Did I feel that my opinion statement was really strong and convincing? Why or why not?
• Which piece of evidence in my paper was strongest? Which was the weakest?
• How difficult was it to find supporting evidence? Will it be easier next time?
• Could my writing have been more convincing? Why or why not?

VOICE

• *Publish your paper for its intended audience.*

How would you describe your voice? Think about the tone and attitude you convey in your paper. Ask yourself if the voice you used really suited both your issue and your audience.

SENTENCE FLUENCY

• *Identify and correct errors in sentence construction.*

This is your last chance to fix any simple sentence construction problems in your paper. Make sure you don't have any run-ons or fragments. Also, check your sentence variety one more time. Have you used the same subject-verb-object construction in every sentence? You might change a few sentences to create some more interesting and varied structures. See pages 13–14 for help with sentence fluency problems.

CONVENTIONS

• *Proofread and edit the paper to catch and correct errors in paragraphing, spelling, capitalization, punctuation and grammar.*

Take care not to let any distracting errors slip into your published paper. Give your paper a final proofread using the convention errors checklist on pages 15–16.

Persuasive Writing Prompts for Practice

Remember, persuasive writing prompts will ask you to state an opinion about an issue and support it with strong reasons. Use the writing process and the six traits to prepare responses to these prompts. Write your responses on your own paper. Use the self-evaluation rubrics on pages 126–132 to evaluate your responses.

Practice Prompts

Prompt 1   Your school district is considering changing school hours so that classes begin and end an hour earlier. Instead of arriving at school at 8:30 and leaving at 2:45, students would attend school from 7:30 to 1:45. Write an essay in which you state an opinion about this change and provide reasons that support your opinion.

Prompt 2   Are dress codes a restriction on personal freedom? Do dress codes at school help maintain discipline and reduce distractions? Write a well-organized paper in which you state and give reasons for your opinion on this issue.

Prompt 3   The local public library wants to shut down every weekday afternoon in order to discourage middle- and high-school students from using the library. Librarians say that the students are noisy and disruptive and use the library only because they have nowhere else to go after school. Should the library be able to close its doors to young people? Write an essay in which you state your opinion and give reasons and details to support it.

Prompt 4   A local business will pay for expensive sports equipment for your school. In return, the school must place ads for the business around the school—in the gymnasium, on the sides of school buses, and in the cafeteria. What is your opinion about this trade-off? Write an essay in which you state an opinion and give reasons to support it.

Prompt 5   Read the quotation below from Roman historian Gaius Sallustius Crispus (c. 86–35/34 B.C.).

"The fame which is based on wealth or beauty is a frail and fleeting thing; but virtue shines for ages with undiminished luster."

Do you agree or disagree with Crispus' thoughts on fame? Write a persuasive essay in which you support or challenge his point of view and give reasons that back up your opinion. Use examples from real life, literature, and the media.

Prompt 6   Think about current events and world issues you have learned about recently. Examples might include climate change, the war on terrorism, or the world's continuing need for resources such as oil and clean water. Which issue do you think is the most pressing—the one you will continue to deal with as you become an adult? Write an essay in which you identify the issue and express an opinion about it. Give reasons that support your opinion and use examples from real life, literature, and the media.

WRITING WORKSHOP III: USING THE SIX TRAITS TO WRITE NARRATIVE TEXT

The purpose of a narrative text is to tell a story. You will retell the events in the order they took place using interesting characters, images, and dialogue. The narrative should have an implied main idea or express a theme—an idea about the human condition.

Narrative texts include fictional narratives, historical narratives, eyewitness accounts, or personal narratives. This workshop will focus on personal narratives. A personal narrative tells a story based on your personal experiences.

(PREWRITING) Prewriting is where you do the work of choosing an experience or event to retell. *Three of the six traits will help you here.*

💭 IDEAS AND CONTENT

• *Explore ideas and choose an event.*
Personal narratives are stories from your past. Think about experiences that you are comfortable sharing with others. You may also want to reread old journal entries or look in photo albums. (For help, see the brainstorming graphic organizer on page 91.)

Quick Tip Personal narrative writing prompts often ask you to write about an experience in which you learned or felt something. Choose an experience that is meaningful but that isn't too personal.

• *Evaluate your ideas.*
Ask yourself some questions: "Will readers find this story interesting?" "Can I tell it neatly and convey its importance?" "Is it an experience that I'm comfortable sharing with others?"

• *Think about your audience and your purpose for writing.*
In a personal narrative, your main purpose is to express yourself by telling about something that happened to you. Your audience will expect you to write in the first person, to tell events in order, and to reveal your feelings. Can your audience handle it? If not, change your topic.

ORGANIZATION

• *Create a time line.*

Most personal narratives are told in chronological order, the order in which events took place. Sometimes, though, flashbacks are fun. They start the story in the middle and "flash back" in time to show the "background. (See the worksheet on page 97.)

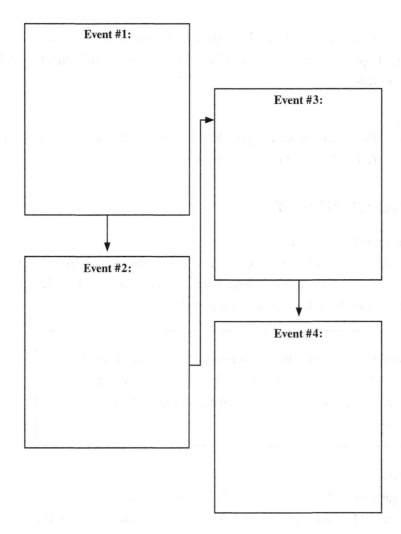

Event #1:

Event #3:

Event #2:

Event #4:

 VOICE

• *Think about your audience. What voice should you use?*

You get to express your individual voice in a personal narrative. Use a voice that suits your narrative. For example, if you are writing about something that happened when you were four, you might use the voice of a young child. For historical narratives or eyewitness accounts, a serious, formal voice is best. (For help with voice, see page 10.)

WRITING Writing is the stage where you put your ideas down on paper. *Five of the six traits will help you here.*

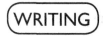 IDEAS AND CONTENT

• *Frame your event.*
Think about where your narrative will begin and where it will end. As you write, also think about the point of the story. Every narrative says something, either directly or indirectly, about the writer or the world. Make sure the details in the middle tell an interesting story.

ORGANIZATION

• *Tell events in the order they happened.*
Use chronological order to tell your story. You can jazz things up by using flashbacks or build suspense by using a flash-forward (telling about events to come), but use these techniques only if they enhance the telling of the narrative. Be sure to set the scene and establish the "characters" early on in the narrative. Make sure the meaning of the experience gets expressed.

VOICE

• *Make sure your voice rings loud and clear.*
Create a voice that sounds natural for the "character" that you are in a personal narrative. If you are young and naïve, your voice should reflect that. If you are a cynical teen, again your voice should reflect those qualities. Personal narratives are one form of writing that really lets a writer discover his or her own voice.

Introduction
• Attention-grabbing beginning
• Details that set the scene

Body
• Event 1 and details
• Event 2 and details (and so on)

Conclusion
• Meaning of the experience for the narrator

WORD CHOICE

• *As you write, choose language that best reflects your characters.*
Narratives include dialogue, which allows characters to speak directly to readers in their own words. Feel free to use slang, informal language, and jargon—if that is what your narrator and characters would use. In descriptive passages, use words that really capture the scene and appeal to readers' five senses.

SENTENCE FLUENCY

• *Play with sentence length and even break the rules.*
In narratives, writers often use sentence fragments to convey what real speech sounds like. Experiment with sentence fragments in your narrative. See how they affect your style and rhythm of writing. Ultimately, though, follow your teacher's guidance about the use of fragments.

| REVISING AND EVALUATING | The revising and evaluating stage is the most important in the process of writing a narrative paper. It is where you figure out if your ideas, organization, and style are working and if you are communicating your ideas clearly. *Five of the six traits will help you here.* |

💭 IDEAS AND CONTENT

• *Evaluate and revise the ideas and content of the paper.*

Have you expressed your key idea clearly? Did you leave out any important details, people, or events? Do readers need any additional background information to understand your narrative?

Have you told too much? Trim out any details that are too personal or take away focus from the most important events. Use the Guidelines for Self-Evaluation on page 86. They will help you decide if you need to edit or revise any of your ideas and content.

🧩 ORGANIZATION

• *Evaluate and revise the organization of the paper.*
Have you told events in a logical order? Use the Guidelines for Self-Evaluation. They will help you decide if you need to change your organizational structure.

🔊 VOICE

• *Refine the style of the paper so that it suits the audience and purpose and conveys the appropriate voice.*
Does your voice engage readers and sound "real"? Is it the right voice for a narrative piece and for this particular story? Do individual characters have their own unique voices, if appropriate? (See page 10 in this book for help with voice.)

WORD CHOICE

• *Evaluate and revise the words you use.*
Your choice of words should make the narrative come alive and make the voice or voices sound real. Read your narrative aloud to see how the dialogue sounds. (Also, see pages 11–12 for help with word choice.)

≈ SENTENCE FLUENCY

• *Evaluate and revise your sentences and paragraphs.*
Make sure your transitional words and phrases are clear. To make your writing more interesting, make sure some of your sentences start with phrases or clauses. (Also, see pages 13–14 for help with sentence fluency.)

Style Guideline *Varying Sentence Lengths*

Variety in sentence length adds rhythm and style. In expository or persuasive writing, you would normally avoid using short, choppy sentences. However, in narrative writing, you may want to use short, choppy sentences for effect. Short, choppy sentences suggest a breathless, suspenseful situation. Long sentences suggest the writer is in complete control.

Short and choppy for suspense:
The doorbell rang. I looked out the side window. I didn't see anyone. It rang again. I answered the door. No one was there! I felt a little freaked out. Who rang the bell? (Do the short, choppy sentences make you feel the writer's tension?)

Combined:
When the doorbell rang, I looked out the side window but didn't see anyone. Then, the doorbell rang again, so I answered the door, but no one was there. I felt a little freaked out because I didn't know who rang the bell. (Does the writer really sound scared when the sentences are combined?)

Guidelines for Self-Evaluation

Evaluation Questions	Tip	Editing/Revision Techniques
IDEAS AND CONTENT 1. Does the beginning grab the audience's attention and set the scene? Does the narrative convey an important message at the end?	**Put stars** next to quotations, surprising details, or statements that would interest the audience. **Circle** details that show when and where the experience happened. **Underline** the writer's statement of why the experience is meaningful.	If needed, **add** a quotation, surprising detail, or interesting statement. **Add** details about when and where the event happened. **Add** a statement that explains the narrative's importance, if necessary.
ORGANIZATION 2. Are the events in chronological order?	**Number** the events as they appear in the paper. **Compare** the numbered events to the actual order of events in time.	**Rearrange** the order of events, if necessary.
VOICE 3. Is the voice in the paper appropriate for the story and the audience?	In the margins, **write** an adjective that describes the voice in the story.	If the tone changes abruptly or does not match the content or the audience, **adjust** word choice and phrasing to make it more appropriate.
WORD CHOICE 4. Do the words used by the narrator and any characters in the narrative sound "true"?	**Circle** all the words or phrases that you think sound "true" to the narrator's voice or to the characters' voices.	If a paragraph has no circled words, **reread** it and see where you can add words or phrases that sound natural. **Consult** a thesaurus to find synonyms that have more flavor.
SENTENCE FLUENCY 5. Do the sentences' lengths create a sense of rhythm and style? Do they convey the writer's emotions?	**Place stars** next to sentences that really create rhythm or style. **Write** the emotion they help convey in the margin.	**Adjust** sentence lengths to create a certain rhythm, emotion, or style.

PUBLISHING Publishing is the stage in the writing process where you make your paper ready for your actual readers. *As you prepare your paper for publication, consider four of the six traits.*

IDEAS AND CONTENT

• *Reflect on your completed paper.*

Consider how you might approach a similar writing assignment next time. Ask yourself the following questions:
• What was the clearest or most exciting detail in my narrative? Why do I think so?
• Was I able to find meaning in my experience as I wrote about it?
• What was the hardest part of writing the narrative—setting the scene? writing the dialogue? creating style with my sentences?

VOICE

• *Publish your paper for its intended audience.*

How would you describe your voice in your narrative? Ask yourself if you were able to create the voice you wanted. Is the voice right for the audience that will actually read your published narrative?

SENTENCE FLUENCY

• *Identify and correct errors in sentence construction.*

This is your last chance to fix any simple sentence construction problems in your paper. For example, you might double-check that you have not used included any stringy sentences or wordy sentences in your narrative. See pages 13–14 for help with sentence fluency problems.

CONVENTIONS

• *Proofread and edit the paper to catch and correct errors in paragraphing, spelling, capitalization, punctuation and grammar.*

Take care not to let any distracting errors slip into your published paper. Give your paper a final proofread using the convention errors checklist on pages 15–16.

Narrative Writing Prompts for Practice

Remember, narrative writing prompts will ask you to tell a story or recall an experience. Use the writing process and the six traits to prepare responses to these prompts. Write your responses on your own paper. Use the self-evaluation rubrics on pages 126–132 to evaluate your responses.

Practice Prompts

Prompt 1   Think of an important event or incident in your life. What lesson did you learn from it? Write a well-developed personal narrative that describes the experience and reveals why it was important to you. Select an event that you feel comfortable sharing with readers.

Prompt 2   Think of a story that has often been retold by your family members or friends. Why is the story so well loved? What does the story reveal about the people in it and the people who tell it? Retell the story in your own words and make sure that the story's significance to your family or friends is clear. Select a story that you feel comfortable sharing with readers.

Prompt 3   Recall a time in your life when you felt your loyalty was being tested. What was that experience like? Write a well-developed personal essay in which you describe the experience and reveal what you learned about yourself and the people in your life. Select an event that you feel comfortable sharing with readers.

Prompt 4   Life is full of "firsts"—the first time you went swimming, the first time you took the bus by yourself, the first time you tasted your favorite food. Select a "first" that was important. In a well-written personal narrative, describe the events that made up this experience. Make sure your narrative makes clear why the event was important or significant. Choose an event you won't mind others reading about.

Prompt 5   Adolescence is a time when young people start to realize that they are unique. How are you unique? Think of an episode from your life in which you realized that you were different from those around you. In a well-written personal narrative, retell the events of that episode. Use dialogue and details to make the experience come alive for readers. Make sure your readers understand what you learned from the experience. Choose an experience you feel comfortable sharing with others.

Prompt 6   Whom do you admire? Think of a person in your life who inspires you to be great. Select an event from that person's life that shows why you think he or she is admirable. In a well-written narrative, describe the episode or event. Make sure that your readers understand why you admire your subject so much. Make sure the person you write about does not mind if you share details about his or her life.

PART FOUR

Worksheets

IDEAS AND CONTENT

Type of Writing: Expository, Persuasive, or Narrative
CLUSTERING: WORD WEB

Directions: Fill in the center circle with a word related to your topic. Then fill in the other circles with related words or ideas. Add more circles, if necessary. Draw lines between the circles to show the connections.

My Topic or Idea

IDEAS AND CONTENT

Type of Writing: Expository, Persuasive, or Narrative
BRAINSTORMING: FREEWRITING

Directions: Use the lines below to write about your topic for about five minutes without stopping. Write down every idea that pops into your head. Don't judge yourself! After your time is up, reread your ideas. Highlight ideas that you want to develop in your paper.

Topic:

_____

_____

_____

_____

_____

_____

_____

_____

_____

_____

_____

_____

_____

_____

_____

_____

_____

_____

_____

Name _____ Date _____

 IDEAS AND CONTENT

Type of Writing: Expository, Persuasive, or Narrative
IDENTIFYING THE MAIN IDEA

Directions: Use the graphic organizer below to refine your thoughts into a main idea. Start at the bottom. Fill in the boxes with details and information. In the box labeled "Main Idea," write the idea that the other boxes support.

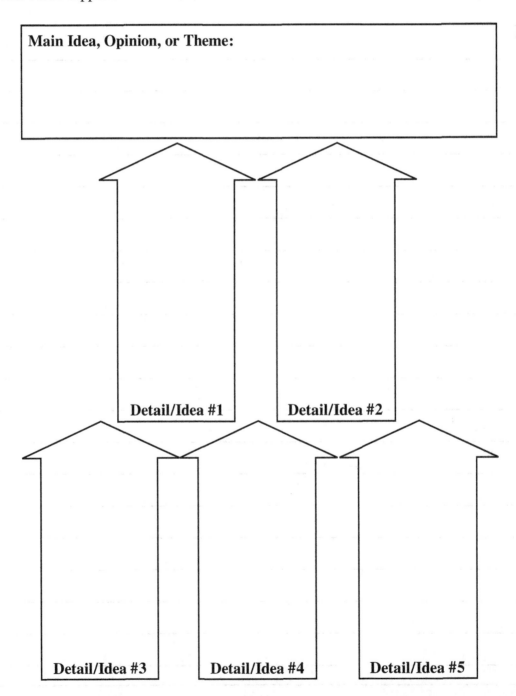

Main Idea, Opinion, or Theme:

Detail/Idea #1

Detail/Idea #2

Detail/Idea #3

Detail/Idea #4

Detail/Idea #5

Name _____   Date _____

 IDEAS AND CONTENT

Type of Writing: Expository, Persuasive, or Narrative
CAUSE AND EFFECT CHAIN

Directions: A cause may have several independent effects. Or, a cause may start a chain reaction, in which one cause leads to an effect, which becomes the cause of another effect. Complete the graphic organizer below to identify causes and effects related to your topic.

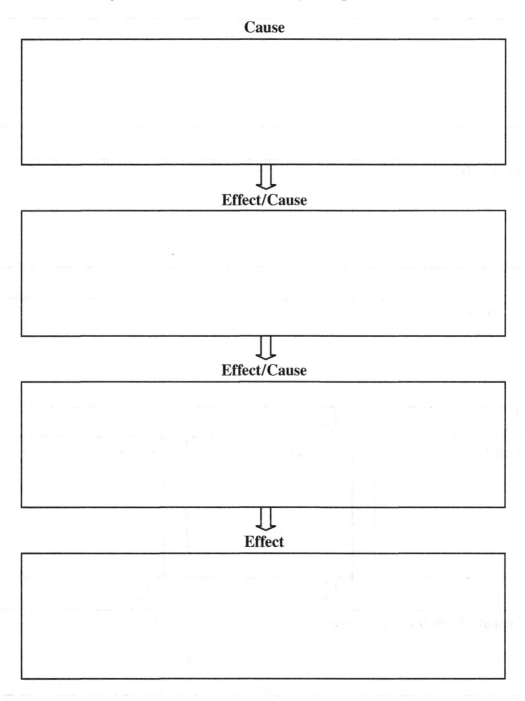

Cause

Effect/Cause

Effect/Cause

Effect

Name _____ Date _____

 IDEAS AND CONTENT

Type of Writing: Narrative
PERSONAL NARRATIVE STORY MAP

Directions: Use the graphic organizer below to identify the main elements of your personal narrative: Setting, Important People, Focus of the Narrative, Events, and What I Learned from the Experience.

Setting:

Where:

When:

⇩

Important People:

⇩

Focus of Narrative:

⇩   ⇩   ⇩

| Event 1: | Event 2: | Event 3: |

⇩   ⇩   ⇩

What I Learned from the Experience:

Name _____ Date _____

 IDEAS AND CONTENT

Type of Writing: Persuasive
PROS AND CONS

Directions: Many topics or issues have both pros (positive arguments or advantages) and cons (negative arguments or disadvantages). Identify the pros and cons associated with your topic or issue.

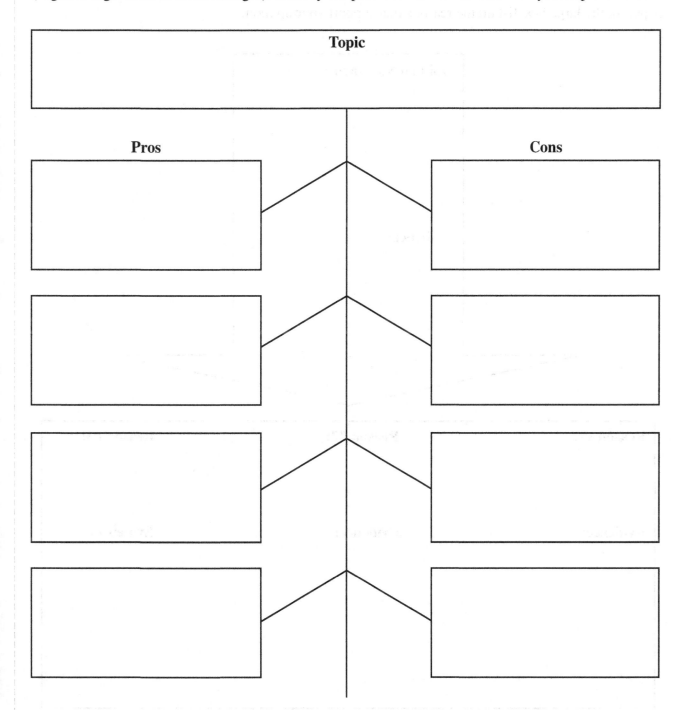

Topic

Pros

Cons

Name _____   Date _____

Type of Writing: Persuasive
STATING AN OPINION

Directions: Use the graphic organizer below to identify an opinion statement and the reasons that support it. In the arrow at the top, write your opinion statement and identify the audience for your paper. In the large box, list all the reasons that support your opinion.

Opinion Statement:

Audience:

Reason #1:	Reason #2:	Reason #3:
Evidence:	Evidence:	Evidence:

Name _____   Date _____

 ORGANIZATION

Type of Writing: Expository, Persuasive, or Narrative
FLOW CHART: CHRONOLOGICAL ORDER

Directions: Complete this flow chart by writing the steps or events in chronological order. Include any details that help describe the steps or events. You may add more boxes or continue the organizer on a separate sheet of paper.

Name _____ Date _____

 ORGANIZATION

Type of Writing: Expository or Persuasive
ORGANIZING YOUR REASONS

Directions: Write your topic sentence (your main idea or opinion statement) in the top box. Write each of your reasons and any supporting details or evidence in the separate boxes below it. Then write your conclusion in the bottom box.

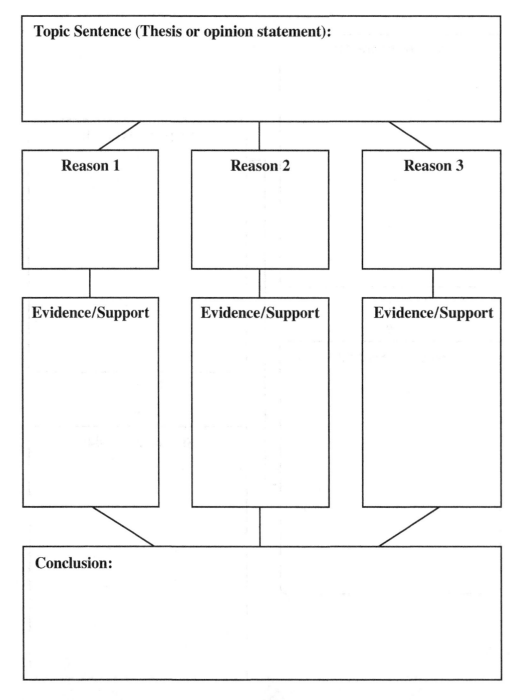

Topic Sentence (Thesis or opinion statement):

Reason 1

Reason 2

Reason 3

Evidence/Support

Evidence/Support

Evidence/Support

Conclusion:

Name _____   Date _____

 ORGANIZATION

Type of Writing: Expository or Persuasive
ORGANIZING REASONS BY ORDER OF IMPORTANCE

Directions: Write your most important reason in the top box. Write your second-most-important reason in the middle box. Write your least important reason in the bottom box. On a separate sheet of paper, try experimenting with a different order, such as least important to most important reason. Which order do you think would work better?

Hint: Most people remember best what they have read last.

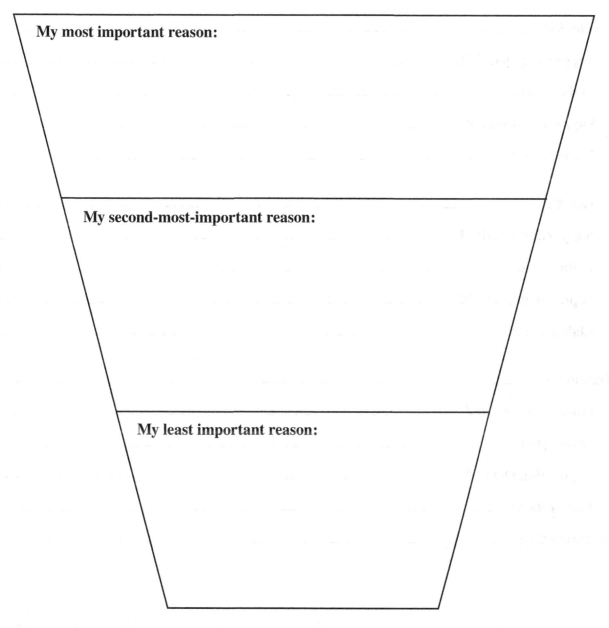

My most important reason:

My second-most-important reason:

My least important reason:

Name _____ Date _____

ORGANIZATION

Type of Writing: Expository or Persuasive
USING AN OUTLINE

Directions: Write each reason in the outline below. Under each reason, write in the supporting details or information. Try to elaborate on each item of support. For example, how does the supporting information prove your point?

Main Idea or Opinion Statement: _____

_____

Reason #1: _____

    Supporting Detail #1: _____

    Elaboration: _____

    Supporting Detail #2: _____

    Elaboration: _____

Reason #2: _____

    Supporting Detail #1: _____

    Elaboration: _____

    Supporting Detail #2: _____

    Elaboration: _____

Reason #3: _____

    Supporting Detail #1: _____

    Elaboration: _____

    Supporting Detail #2: _____

    Elaboration: _____

Summing It Up: _____

Name _____ Date _____

 VOICE

Type of Writing: Expository, Persuasive, or Narrative
IDENTIFYING TONE

Directions: Read each passage below. Then choose one or more of the words from the box at the bottom of the page to identify the tone of the passage. (Or choose tone words of your own.) Write the word or words on the line, along with a statement that explains why you selected that tone.

Passage 1   Requiring students to volunteer or to complete community service in order to graduate is really unfair. While I understand how important it is to give back to the community, I would like to point out that many students already do that—and without getting one bit of credit. Many of my friends help the community through scouting and church groups. They plant trees, clean up playgrounds, and take meals to seniors. To expect them to take on additional community service is just plain unfair.

I would describe the tone as _____ because _____.

Passage 2   Of course everyone loves animals! Duh! Some people like dogs, some like cats, and some like rats. Whatever. You probably own a couple of animals yourself. And why not? After all, scientists and researchers have discovered that pets help lower people's blood pressure and reduce their anxieties. They say that pets are as good as a yoga class. Me? I've got three dogs and no worries—except, of course, where's the leash?

I would describe the tone as _____ because _____.

Passage 3   An ink-cartridge recycling program can help improve our environment. By reusing those little plastic cases, we can keep them out of our landfills. By keeping them out of the dump, we also keep toxic chemicals in the ink from leaking into the ground and into our water supplies. Some stores and ink-cartridge suppliers are dragging their feet, however, and it is up to consumers to light a fire under them and get them to take responsibility for their products.

I would describe the tone as _____ because _____.

reasonable	whiny	respectful	friendly	formal
informal	cheeky	conversational	thoughtful	mean

On Your Own. Now try your skills to create a distinct voice. Choose one of the passages above and rewrite it in a different voice, or tone. Rewrite your passage on a separate sheet of paper. Be prepared to describe the tone you have used.

WORD CHOICE

Type of Writing: Expository, Persuasive, or Narrative
RECOGNIZING CONNOTATIONS

Directions: Use a dictionary and the sample sentences given to determine the definitions and connotations of the words in the first column of the chart below. The first row of the chart gives you an example.

Word	Definition	Sample Sentence	Connotation (Revised Definition)
dawdle	to waste time	After school the children dawdled on the playground.	When you dawdle, you waste time in a pleasant and harmless way.
1. naughty		The naughty puppy barked and then fell off the cushion it was chewing on.	
2. challenging		Lauren found the extra-credit section on the test to be particularly challenging.	
3. oozed		For weeks after the flood, the ground oozed under our feet.	
4. recognition		At his retirement, the teacher received the recognition he deserved.	
5. sensitive		Margot is so sensitive that she gets her feelings hurt all the time.	

On Your Own. Use the words in the chart above in sentences of your own. Write your sentences on a separate sheet of paper. Then explain how the words' connotations affected the way you used them.

Name _____ Date _____

 WORD CHOICE

Type of Writing: Expository, Persuasive, or Narrative
AVOIDING LOADED LANGUAGE, JARGON, AND CLICHÉS

Directions: Read each sentence below. Underline the loaded language, jargon, or cliché (or tired word) that appears in each sentence. On the line provided, write **LL** for loaded language, **J** for jargon, or **C** for cliché or tired word. (See pages 11–12 for help with these terms.)

_____ 1. Mr. Johnson really let the cat out of the bag when he told Linda about the surprise party.

_____ 2. How can honest, hard-working Americans compete in a global economy?

_____ 3. Dennis will run the numbers again to find the error.

_____ 4. Bonnie looked as pretty as a picture for her graduation photo.

_____ 5. After our trip to the beach, my face was as red as a lobster.

_____ 6. Wall Street had a good day today—both the Dow and NASDAQ were up.

_____ 7. After you log on, enter your password and your PIN.

_____ 8. Hospitals are full of quacks who don't know their stethoscopes from their elbows.

_____ 9. Nina really hit the roof when she realized she missed the application date.

_____ 10. An encounter with an incompetent bureaucrat can waste your whole day.

_____ 11. Scan the bar code and see what price comes up.

_____ 12. That can was as flat as a pancake after the bus ran over it.

_____ 13. Your dress is great! It's very unique!

_____ 14. Those fat cat politicians are trying to raise our taxes again.

_____ 15. You can't possibly expect to get good food at a restaurant that caters to wannabes and posers like this one does.

On Your Own. Choose ten sentences from the exercise above and rewrite them without the loaded language, jargon, or cliché. Write your sentences on a separate sheet of paper and review them with a friend.

Name _____ Date _____

 SENTENCE FLUENCY

Type of Writing: Expository, Persuasive, or Narrative
AVOIDING PASSIVE VOICE

Directions: On the short line before each sentence, identify the voice in the sentence as **AV** for active voice or **PV** for passive voice. If a sentence is in passive voice, rewrite it in active voice on the line provided.

_____ 1. The tennis ball was served by Sharmaine.

_____

_____ 2. Dad cooked lasagna for the family last night.

_____

_____ 3. The class was attended by several new people.

_____

_____ 4. The art in the museum is viewed by many tourists.

_____

_____ 5. Our pecan tree was pruned by a tree trimmer.

_____

_____ 6. The dog was given its rabies vaccination by the veterinarian.

_____

_____ 7. The computer was fixed by the technician.

_____

_____ 8. Glenna gave a lecture on her visit to the Southwest.

_____

_____ 9. Her parents praised her for her good attitude.

_____

_____ 10. The plants for the school garden were donated by a local nursery.

_____

_____ 11. Officer Gillman spoke to students about the new curfew.

_____

_____ 12. The package was delivered by the postal worker.

_____

Name _____   Date _____

SENTENCE FLUENCY

Type of Writing: Expository, Persuasive, or Narrative
REVISING PASSIVE VOICE

Directions: Passive voice is often indicated by the use of "to be" verbs. Read the passage below and underline all the "to be" verbs. Then decide if the verbs are helping verbs that create a passive voice. On the lines below, rewrite the paragraph, putting all the sentences in active voice.

The arctic tundra is characterized by long winters, little snow, and low temperatures. Warm summer temperatures thaw the tundra's surface soil but not the subsoil, or permafrost. Therefore, drainage is hindered by flat and partially frozen ground. Ponds and bogs are formed by standing water. Typical arctic vegetation includes low plants, such as cotton grass, sedge, and lichens. Soil disturbances such as "flowing soil" are caused by thaws and movement of soil. Irregular landforms, such as hummocks, frost boils, and earth stripes, are produced by poorly drained areas. On the soft surface, deep gullies are caused by vehicle tracks. Most arctic vegetation can survive these soil disturbances. Likewise, arctic wildlife is also not deeply affected by these changes.

_____

_____

_____

_____

_____

_____

_____

_____

_____

SENTENCE FLUENCY

Type of Writing: Expository, Persuasive, or Narrative
REVISING FOR SENTENCE VARIETY

Directions: The sentences in the paragraphs below all have a similar construction and are roughly the same length. They sound rather dull. On a separate sheet of paper, rewrite and revise the paragraphs by combining sentences to vary the lengths and by beginning some sentences with phrases and clauses. There is no one correct way to revise the paragraphs.

The Populist movement was an American movement. It developed in the 1800s. It began during the depression of the late 1870s. Farmers were losing money then. They formed organized groups. The groups were called Farmers' Alliances. Members of the alliances worked together. They built barns. The barns stored the crops. The crops stayed in the barns until the prices were better. Some alliances included African American farmers. African American farmers could not vote. The alliances welcomed them anyway.

The alliances became powerful at the end of the century. They formed a national political party. They joined forces with another group. It was called the Knights of Labor. The two groups formed the People's Party. Its members were known as Populists. Populists wanted the national government to change. They wanted it to print more paper money. More paper money might raise farm prices. The Populists also wanted a national income tax. Americans did not pay income tax then. It was not a popular idea. Income tax became a reality though. Congress passed an amendment in 1913. It was the sixteenth amendment. It made a national income tax legal. Americans have paid income tax ever since.

Name _____ Date _____

SENTENCE FLUENCY

Type of Writing: Expository, Persuasive, or Narrative
REVISING RUN-ON SENTENCES

Directions: Correct the run-on sentences in the following paragraphs by inserting periods and capital letters where needed. Cross out each incorrect comma or lowercase letter and write the correct period or capital letter above it. Make sure you don't create any sentence fragments! (See page 13 for help.)

Example: *Our local weatherman is very knowledgeable, he has a degree in meteorology.*

Today when modern meteorologists forecast the weather, they can count on the help of an impressive battery of scientific devices. Weather satellites, for example, relay photographs of cloud formations from all over the world these pictures show where storms are beginning over oceans and deserts the paths of typhoons and hurricanes are tracked the same way. Weather information from all sources is fed into powerful computers, thus the weather can be evaluated with amazing speed.

Our ancestors had no complicated weather instruments they had to rely on their eyes and ears and a few old proverbs and maxims. Their methods were hardly scientific today, for example, no one still believes the old superstition about the groundhog, but we celebrate Groundhog Day just the same. The story goes that if the groundhog sees its shadow on the second day of February, there will be six more weeks of winter, watch for yourself and see! The behavior of insects, on the other hand, is still a good indicator of temperature because they are cold blooded. Grasshoppers cannot fly when the temperature drops below 55 degrees Fahrenheit if you hear a cricket chirping, count the number of chirps in fourteen seconds and add forty, then you will have the temperature in degrees Fahrenheit.

Today weather forecasting is much more accurate if less charming than it was in the old days, however, the forecasters are still not always right, perhaps because there are so many factors to consider.

SENTENCE FLUENCY

Type of Writing: Expository, Persuasive, or Narrative
REVISING STRINGY SENTENCES

Directions: The sentences in the paragraph below are stringy. On the lines below, rewrite and revise the stringy sentences by breaking them into two or more sentences or by turning some of the independent clauses into phrases or subordinate clauses. You may add, change, or delete words.

Argentina is a country in South America and it borders the south Atlantic and its capital is Buenos Aires. My friend Leela has been to Argentina, but she went with her family, and her father studied at a university there, but Leela had a great time meeting people, and she got to speak in Spanish. Leela spent time in the city, but she also got to go to the countryside and she learned about the life of the cowboys of South America and she was very impressed. Leela wrote a story about her experiences and it is about a character named Tanmoor, and he is an interesting character, but he is from a small town in Argentina, but he wants to move to the big city. The story has an interesting beginning and it opens with Tanmoor's father working on a ranch but he is a vaquero—a cowboy—and the bank wants to put him out of business, and Tanmoor is trying to help save the ranch. Leela clearly did lots of research and she asked a lot of questions and it shows and the story is excellent!

_____

_____

_____

_____

_____

_____

_____

_____

SENTENCE FLUENCY

Type of Writing: Expository, Persuasive, or Narrative
REVISING WORDY SENTENCES

Directions: The sentences in the paragraph below are wordy. On the lines below, rewrite and revise the wordy sentences by replacing a group of words with a word, using a phrase instead of a clause, or by taking out unnecessary words.

When the daughters of pioneers were young girls, they learned how to sew and cook. Young girls had to learn household skills due to the fact that if they didn't do the chores, the chores wouldn't get done. So girls would attend their mother's instructions with great carefulness and thoughtfulness. They had to do all sorts of chores of the kind that we don't even do anymore, like make butter, bake bread, and wash clothes by hand. Today we have machines, which are convenient and easy to use, to do chores that are related to the household. Also in addition, we never have to cook because we can go to the grocery store and buy any kind of food we want, which is already cooked and ready-to-eat. What I mean to say is that life was hard for pioneer women, and we should be grateful that we can just flip a switch, which is so easy, and get so many jobs done right away and immediately.

_____

_____

_____

_____

_____

_____

_____

_____

_____

Name _____   Date _____

 SENTENCE FLUENCY

Type of Writing: Expository, Persuasive, or Narrative
CHOPPY SENTENCES AND SENTENCE COMBINING

Directions: On the lines provided, combine the choppy sentences into one complete sentence by inserting words or phrases or by using conjunctions.

Example: Mount Everest is famous. It is the most famous mountain in the world.
Mount Everest is the most famous mountain in the world.

1. The Himalayas are mountains in Asia. They are the tallest mountains in Asia.

   _____

   _____

2. Tea bushes grow on slopes. The slopes are on the hills near Darjeeling. The slopes are steep. The hills are fertile.

   _____

   _____

3. The danger in climbing is great. It comes from the altitude and the cold. The altitude is high. The cold is bitter.

   _____

   _____

4. Marissa's family will hike in Rocky Mountain National Park. They will pitch tents. The tents will be pitched in Hidden Valley.

   _____

   _____

5. Mrs. Goldstein jogs every morning. She jogs in the park. She walks her dog every evening.

   _____

   _____

6. Bruce received a beautiful wall hanging. It was from his grandmother in Vietnam.

   _____

   _____

7. Helga bought new shoes. The shoes were for running. She bought them during the sale.

   _____

   _____

Name _____ Date _____

 # SENTENCE FLUENCY

Type of Writing: Expository, Persuasive, or Narrative
USING TRANSITIONAL WORDS AND PHRASES

To show readers how ideas are connected, writers use transitional words and phrases.

Chronological Order	after, at last, at once, before, eventually, finally, first, later, meanwhile, next, soon, then, when, while
Cause and Effect	as a result, because, consequently, for, for this reason, since, so, so that, therefore
Spatial Order	above, across, among, around, before, behind, below, beneath, by, down, here, in, inside, into, near, next to, over, there, under, up
Order of Importance	first, last, mainly, more important, then, to begin with
Comparison	also, and, another, just as, like, likewise, moreover, similarly, too
Contrast	although, but, however, in spite of, instead, nevertheless, on the other hand, otherwise, still, yet

Directions: Read the passage below and underline all the transitional words and phrases you can find.

After dinner, we sang songs around the campfire and told stories. As the cool night air arrived, I pulled out my sleeping bag and unrolled it. Then Jeb and I took the pails down to the stream and filled them. We set them beside the fire and waited. Meanwhile everyone seemed to be dozing off. When I was certain that everyone was asleep, I used the water in the bucket to douse the fire. The hot logs sizzled as a result of being splashed with cold water.

Then I climbed into my sleeping bag and looked at the stars above me. Although I had spent a lot of time in the country, I had trouble remembering the formal names of the constellations. My father had tried to teach me, but I forgot. So I invented my own names, and I remembered them, too. Eventually I fell asleep and dreamed I could float in the sky like the stars.

The next morning, the first thing I did was restart the fire. I knew the campers would never forgive me if they had to wait for their breakfasts. More important, I did not want to wait long for my first cup of coffee. Otherwise I would be very grumpy.

On Your Own. Identify five transitional words or phrases in the passage. Explain how the transitions connect ideas. Write your explanations on a separate sheet of paper.

CONVENTIONS

Type of Writing: Expository, Persuasive, or Narrative
PARAGRAPHING

Directions: Read the paragraph below. Decide where the paragraph should be divided into three paragraphs. Draw a slash mark (/) to indicate where the breaks should occur. On the lines at the bottom of the page, explain why you started the new paragraphs where you did.

I have heard people talking about the proposed youth recreation center, and I believe that it is a fine idea. While some adults may think homework and chores are enough to keep students busy after school, there are still a few hours each afternoon when many of us are bored and restless. The youth center would take care of our needs to find safe, fun things to do. Those who don't agree with the plans for the center seem to think that young people always have another kid or two to do things with in our free time. That is not always the case. Since students have different schedules during the weekday afternoons and weekends, it is not always possible to find someone who is free. Sometimes I am actually lonely after school but don't want to just walk around downtown. There are people there who could get me into trouble. I want to avoid that type of crowd and find a safe place to hang out. My parents both have full-time jobs and would be glad if there were a youth center I could go to after school. Finally, I believe that there is a lot I can learn from the youth center programs. I have heard that such programs can offer games, singing groups, arts and crafts activities, and job counseling for older kids. These centers are also good places to make friends.

_____

_____

_____

_____

_____

_____

Name _____ Date _____

 CONVENTIONS

Type of Writing: Expository, Persuasive, or Narrative
USAGE: VERB AGREEMENT

Directions: Underline the subject of each sentence and the italicized verb in parentheses that agrees with the subject.

1. My sisters never (*enjoy, enjoys*) ice skating anymore.

2. The club members (*is, are*) planning an overnight hike.

3. No one but Jacqueline (*want, wants*) to go.

4. The local newspaper (*doesn't, don't*) print much foreign news.

5. Anybody who is interested in boats (*need, needs*) to know how to swim.

6. Neither of my grandmothers (*has, have*) retired.

7. Few of the documents (*was, were*) authentic.

8. Not one of the astronomers (*know, knows*) whether life exists on Mars.

9. Among writers, some (*has, have*) made predictions that came true.

10. A fleet of ships (*are, is*) sailing into the harbor.

11. Deneice and Maria (*play, plays*) volleyball after school.

12. Neither Ellie nor Noah (*read, reads*) much science fiction.

13. Ms. Galinsky or Mr. Wilson (*have, has*) the details about the meeting.

14. (*Has, Have*) the committee checked the date for its next meeting?

15. (*Don't, Doesn't*) the falling rain sound beautiful?

16. The dogs (*wag, wags*) their tails with excitement.

17. Flocks of birds (*fly, flies*) over our house on their way south for winter.

18. Bottles of water (*was, were*) waiting for the runners at the finish line.

19. Some of the puzzle pieces (*is, are*) straight on one edge.

20. Which sandwiches (*has, have*) only peanut butter on them?

21. During the summer, all of the beaches (*is, are*) crowded with tourists.

22. Frank and Sarah's new car (*run, runs*) on electricity.

23. The flags around the ballpark (*wave, waves*) in the breeze.

24. The scent of the roses in the field (*fill, fills*) the air.

25. The rocks (*gain, gains*) speed as they roll down the hillside.

Name _____ Date _____

 CONVENTIONS

Type of Writing: Expository, Persuasive, or Narrative
USAGE: VERB TENSE

Directions: In the following paragraph, the verb tenses are not consistent. Decide whether the paragraph should be in the present or the past tense. Then, on the lines below, rewrite the paragraph, making sure to use consistent tense.

    Eleanor Roosevelt's parents died when she was a child, so she is raised by her grandmother and sent to school in England. There she fell under the influence of headmistress Marie Souvestre, who works for social causes. As a young adult, Roosevelt participated in social work before she marries Franklin Delano Roosevelt. After her husband enters politics, she works for the American Red Cross during World War I and later became more involved in politics herself. In the early 1930s, Mrs. Roosevelt becomes a leading activist for women's rights. When her husband was elected President of the United States, Mrs. Roosevelt helps other women get appointed to government positions. She travels around the country, visited coal mines and slums, and speaks out for the poor. After her husband's death, Mrs. Roosevelt is appointed by President Truman to be a delegate to the United Nations. Her service to the U.N. is probably her greatest achievement. Roosevelt devoted her whole life to causes of humanity and is loved by many.

_____

_____

_____

_____

_____

_____

_____

Name _____ Date _____

 CONVENTIONS

Type of Writing: Expository, Persuasive, or Narrative
STANDARD USAGE

Directions: Underline the word or expression in parentheses that is correct according to the standards for formal usage.

1. More people could (*have, of*) gone to the game if it hadn't rained.

2. That perfume smells really (*bad, badly*).

3. No one really knows the (*affects, effects*) the new discovery will have.

4. There is (*fewer, less*) water in the local lakes because of the drought.

5. Tasha, why did you give (*them, those*) sweaters away?

6. We are fortunate to be able to (*choose, chose*) which classes to take.

7. Did you read (*that, where*) the pool will close early on Saturday?

8. Dad and I will (*try and, try to*) pull up all the weeds today.

9. We noticed that the twins helped (*theirselves, themselves*) to extra helpings.

10. When Nora is sad, she becomes (*real, very*) quiet.

11. The company report concludes that there (*ain't, isn't*) much demand for wigs.

12. Probably everyone (*accept, except*) Eliza is hoping for more snow.

13. Did Aaron tell you (*how come, why*) he didn't go to practice?

14. Sheryl's backpack zipper (*broke, busted*) as she walked to school.

15. The chores were divided equally (*among, between*) the three children.

16. The plant wilted in the sun and still does not look (*good, well*).

17. (*A, An*) gila monster, a type of desert lizard, isn't actually a monster.

18. The reason we have no e-mail is (*because, that*) the server is down.

19. Gretchen talked (*as if, like*) she wanted to go to the beach with us tomorrow.

20. In our school, country music is more popular (*than, then*) classical music.

21. (*Advertisers, Advertisers they*) often use exaggeration in their commercials.

22. Lola is not sure where Grafton Street (*is, is at*).

23. Ms. Brown tried to (*learn, teach*) the eighth-graders about prime numbers.

24. To our astonishment, the ball landed (*outside, outside of*) the line.

25. After the repair, the car's performance improved (*some, somewhat*).

Name _____ Date _____

 CONVENTIONS

Type of Writing: Expository, Persuasive, or Narrative
CAPITALIZATION AND SPELLING

Directions: Circle the letters that should be capitalized in the following paragraph. Draw a slash through capital letters that should be lowercase.

America's food has been influenced by many Cultures. Who has not enjoyed chinese Egg drop soup, italian pasta, mexican tacos, or the german and scandinavian Cheeses from wisconsin. The smorgasbord may seem american, but the idea originated in sweden. Pretzels were originally dutch delicacies. Shish Kebab, which is often served at backyard Barbecues, is actually a Turkish dish. No thanksgiving dinner would be complete without Turkey, corn, and pumpkin. These foods are truly American, for they were here long before the Pilgrims reached north America.

Directions: The following paragraph contains fifteen spelling errors. For each sentence, draw a line through any misspelled word and write the correct spelling above it.

The Regional Art Club includes members from middle schools in twenty-two citys. Art critics throughout the state conceed that our members are extremely talented. "Use your imagination" and "Express your creativeity" are our mottos. We have large studioes at four centrally located schools. There is a large vareity of artistic stiles among our members. Some students make huge sculpturs out of mettal objects. The club is overun with painters, as you might expect. Potters easyly come in secund in number. Photogaphy is also a poplar art, especially with many students in the nineth grade. Members usually meet once during the week and agin on Saturdays.

CONVENTIONS

Type of Writing: Expository, Persuasive, or Narrative
PUNCTUATION

Directions: Read the passage below and add commas, semicolons, colons, and end marks where they are needed.

One hundred years ago there were a hundred thousand elephants living in Asia however, now

there are only about one third of that number What an alarming loss The Asian elephant is now

an endangered species for the following reasons cutting of forests other damage to habitat and

increased human population Of the Asian elephants that remain about ten thousand live in the

small country of Myanmar Can you find the country in the atlas It is located between Thailand and

Bangladesh Many of the huge patient elephants also called timber elephants work with humans

together they bring in large valuable trees to sell for lumber The elephants and the people have

a partnership and they spend their lives together This partnership is remarkable for the mutual

affection and trust it demonstrates between animals and humans

Directions: Read the passage below. Cross out any incorrect punctuation and add any punctuation marks that have been omitted.

I propose that the group take a canoe trip down the Delaware said Nicky with enthusiasm! We

could rent canoes in Callicoon and paddle down to Bingham Falls.

I think that is a good idea Charlotte replied but how do we get the canoes back to Callicoon.

Thats easy Nicky answered because there is a series of posts along the river where we can leave

the canoes. We rent them at one post and check them at a post farther down the river.

Lets schedule the trip for next weekend Bryce exclaimed.

CONVENTIONS

Type of Writing: Expository, Persuasive, or Narrative
PROOFREADING: CHECKLIST AND CHART

Directions: Proofreading your own writing means checking it for mistakes in grammar, usage, spelling, capitalization, and punctuation. Use the following guidelines to help you review either your own or another student's writing. Then, create a chart like the one below to record any errors that you find.

1. Is every sentence complete?

2. Does every sentence begin with a capital letter? Are proper nouns capitalized?

3. Does every sentence end with the correct punctuation mark?

4. Do subjects and verbs agree?

5. Are verbs in the right form and tense?

6. Are adjective and adverb forms used correctly in making comparisons?

7. Are the forms of personal pronouns used correctly?

8. Does every pronoun agree with its antecedent (the word it refers to) in number and gender? Are pronoun references clear?

9. Are all words spelled correctly?

10. Is the writing neat and legible?

Error Log

Grammar and Usage	
Description of Problem(s)	Location (Page and Line)
Spelling	
Misspelled Words	Correct Spellings
Capitalization	
Words with Errors	Corrections
Punctuation	
Description of Problem(s)	Location (Page and Line)

PART FIVE

Rubrics and Answer Key

TEACHER/EVALUATOR

SIX TRAITS RUBRIC: IDEAS AND CONTENT

Score 5	It's Crystal Clear!
A Score 5 paper is clear, focused, and interesting. It presents relevant and concrete details that catch and maintain the reader's interest and support a clear main idea, theme, or story line.	√ The topic is clearly focused—neither too broad nor too narrow—for a paper of its kind. √ The ideas are original, interesting, and creative. √ The writer draws from personal experience or knowledge. √ Key details are insightful and well chosen; they are not obvious, predictable, or clichéd. √ The development of the topic is thorough and logical; the writer anticipates and answers the reader's questions. √ Supporting details are accurate and relevant; every detail contributes to the whole.
Score 3	**Close—It's Getting There.**
A Score 3 paper develops the topic in a general or basic way. Although clear, the ideas in the paper are routine and lack insight.	√ The topic is underdeveloped, but readers can still understand the writer's purpose and predict how ideas will develop. √ Supporting details are present but can be vague and do not help illustrate the main idea or theme; the writer refers to his or her own experience or knowledge but often fails to push beyond the obvious to more specific ideas. √ Ideas are understandable but not detailed, elaborated upon, or personalized; the writer's ideas do not reveal deep comprehension of the topic or of the writing task. √ The writer does not stray from the topic, but the ideas remain general, forcing readers to rely on what they already know to make sense of the paper; more information is needed to create a complete picture.
Score 1	**Hmm. What Is the Writer Trying to Say?**
A Score 1 paper fails to exhibit any clear purpose or main idea. The reader must infer a coherent and meaningful message from scattered details and incomplete observations.	√ The writer appears not to have decided on a topic or main idea; the paper reads like a rough draft or brainstorming notes; it is full of random thoughts. √ The thesis is a vague statement about the topic or a restatement of a prompt, with little or no support, detail, or insight. √ Information is limited and spotty; readers must make inferences to make connections or to identify any organizational pattern. √ The text is rambling and repetitious; ideas are underdeveloped; the paper is too short. √ The paper lacks subordination of ideas; every idea and detail seems equally weighted; ideas are not tied to an overarching thesis or theme.

TEACHER/EVALUATOR

SIX TRAITS RUBRIC: ORGANIZATION

Score 5	Yes! I Can See Where This Is Going.
A Score 5 paper uses organizational patterns to clearly communicate a central idea or story line. The order of information draws the reader effortlessly through the text.	√ The paper employs a logical and effective sequence of ideas. √ The paper contains both an attention-grabbing introduction and a satisfying conclusion. √ The pacing is carefully controlled; the writer slows down to provide explanation or elaboration when appropriate and increases the pace when necessary. √ Transitions make clear connections and cue the reader to specific relationships between ideas. √ The organizational structure is appropriate to the writer's purpose and audience. √ If present, the title sums up the central idea of the paper in a fresh and thoughtful way.
Score 3	**Close—Wait, I Think I Get It.**
A Score 3 paper is reasonably strong; it enables readers to move forward without too much confusion.	√ The paper has an introduction and a conclusion. However, the introduction may not be engaging, and the conclusion may not knit together all the paper's ideas. √ The sequence is logical but predictable and therefore not very compelling. √ The sequence may not consistently support the paper's ideas; readers may reorder sections mentally or provide transitions as they read. √ Pacing is reasonably well done, although the writer may move ahead too quickly or linger over unimportant ideas. √ Transitions between ideas may be unclear. √ If present, the title may be dull or lacking insight.
Score 1	**Hmm. I'm a Little Lost.**
A Score 1 paper fails to exhibit a sense of purpose or writing strategy; ideas, details, or events seem to be cobbled together without any internal structure or flow.	√ The sequence is broken; one idea or event does not logically follow another; lack of organizational structure, such as clear paragraph breaks, makes it difficult for readers to understand the progression of ideas or events. √ The paper lacks both a clear introduction to guide readers and a conclusion that sums up ideas at the end. √ Pacing is halting or inconsistent; the writer appears not to know when to slow down or speed up the pace. √ Transitions between ideas are confusing or absent. √ If present, the title does not accurately reflect the content of the paper.

TEACHER/EVALUATOR

SIX TRAITS RUBRIC: VOICE

Score 5	Yes! I Can Really Hear You.
A Score 5 paper is engaging and conveys the writer's awareness of audience and purpose.	√ The tone of the writing is appropriate for the purpose and audience of the paper. √ The reader is aware of and feels connected to a real person behind the text; if appropriate, the writer takes risks in revealing a personal dimension throughout the piece. √ If the paper is expository or persuasive, the writer shows a strong connection to the topic and explains why readers should care about the issue. √ If the paper is narrative, the point of view is sincere, interesting, and compelling.
Score 3	**Close. Try Again With Feeling.**
A Score 3 paper is reasonably genuine but does not reveal any excitement or connection with the issue; the resulting paper is pleasant but not truly engaging.	√ The writer offers generalities instead of personal insights; as a result, the writing feels impersonal. √ The writer uses neutral language and a flat tone. √ The writer communicates in an earnest and pleasing manner yet takes no risks; the reader does not feel inspired or engaged. √ Expository or persuasive writing does not reveal the writer's engagement with the topic; there is no attempt to build credibility with the audience. √ Narrative writing fails to reveal a fresh or individual perspective.
Score 1	**Hmm. I Can Barely Hear You.**
A Score 1 paper is mechanical or wooden. The writer appears indifferent to the topic and the audience.	√ The writer shows no concern with the audience; the voice may be inappropriate for the intended reader. √ The development of the topic is so limited that no identifiable point of view is present, or the writing is so short that it offers little but a general introduction of the topic. √ The writer seems to speak in a monotone, using a voice that suppresses all excitement about the message or topic. √ Although the writing may communicate on a functional level, it is ordinary and takes no risks. √ Expository or persuasive writing may lack accurate information or use overly technical language. Narrative writing may lack a point of view and fail to inspire interest.

TEACHER/EVALUATOR

SIX TRAITS RUBRIC: WORD CHOICE

Score 5	Yes! Your Words Come Through Loud and Clear.
In a Score 5 paper, words are precise, engaging, and natural. They convey the writer's message in an interesting and effective way.	√ All words are specific and appropriate. In all instances, the writer has taken care to choose the right words or phrases. √ The paper's language is natural, not overdone; it never shows a lack of control. Clichés and jargon are rarely used. √ The paper contains energetic verbs; precise nouns and modifiers provide clarity. √ The writer uses vivid words and phrases, including sensory details; such language creates distinct images in the reader's mind.
Score 3	Close—With a Little Polish Your Words Will Shine.
Despite its lack of flair, the writing in a Score 3 paper gets the message across because it is functional and clear.	√ Words are correct and generally adequate but lack originality or precision. √ Familiar words and phrases do not grab the reader's interest or imagination. Occasional use of lively verbs and phrases perks things up, but the language does not consistently sparkle. √ Attempts at engaging or academic language may seem showy or overdone. √ The writing contains passive verbs and basic nouns and adjectives, and it lacks precise adverbs.
Score 1	Hmm. I Don't Understand What You Mean.
The limited vocabulary in a Score 1 paper prevents readers from understanding the writer's message. The writer's struggle for words keeps readers from making connections.	√ Vague language communicates an imprecise or incomplete message or understanding of the topic. The reader feels confused and unsure of the writer's purpose. √ Words are used incorrectly. In addition, frequent misuse of parts of speech limits readers' comprehension. √ Excessive repetition distracts readers from the message. √ The writing overuses jargon or clichés.

TEACHER/EVALUATOR

SIX TRAITS RUBRIC: SENTENCE FLUENCY

Score 5	Yes! The Sentences Really Flow.
Sentences in a Score 5 paper are thoughtfully constructed, and sentence structure is varied throughout. When read aloud, the writing is fluent and rhythmic.	√ The writer constructs sentences so that meaning is clear to the reader. √ Sentences vary in length and in structure. √ Varied sentence beginnings add interest and clarity. √ The writing has a steady rhythm; the reader is able to read the text effortlessly without confusion or stumbling. √ Dialogue, if used, is natural. Any fragments are used purposefully and contribute to the paper's style. √ Thoughtful connectives and transitions between sentences reveal how the paper's ideas work together.
Score 3	**Close—But I Feel As Though I'm Drifting Off Course.**
Text of a Score 3 paper maintains a steady rhythm, but the reader may find it flat or mechanical rather than fluent or musical.	√ Sentences are usually grammatical and unified, but they are routine rather than artful. The writer has not paid a great deal of attention to how the sentences sound. √ There is some variation in sentence length and structure as well as in sentence beginnings. Not all sentences are constructed exactly the same way. √ The reader may have to search for transitional words and phrases that show how sentences relate to one another. Sometimes, such context clues are entirely absent when they should be present. √ Although sections of the paper invite expressive oral reading, the reader may also encounter many stilted or awkward sections.
Score 1	**Hmm. I'm a Little Lost.**
The reader of a Score 1 paper will encounter challenges in reading the choppy or confusing text; meaning may be significantly obscured by the errors in sentence construction.	√ The sentences do not "hang together." They are run-on, incomplete, monotonous, or awkward. √ Phrasing often sounds too singsong, not natural. The paper does not allow for expressive oral reading. √ Nearly all the sentences begin the same way, and they may all follow the same pattern (e.g., subject-verb-object). The end result may be a monotonous repetition of sounds. √ Endless connectives or a complete lack of connectives creates a confused muddle of language.

TEACHER/EVALUATOR

SIX TRAITS RUBRIC: CONVENTIONS

Score 5	It's Nearly Perfect!
In a Score 5 paper, standard writing conventions are used correctly and in a way that aids the reader's understanding. Any errors tend to be minor; the piece is nearly ready for publication.	√ Paragraphing is regular and enhances the organization of the paper. √ Grammar and usage are correct and add clarity to the text as a whole. Sometimes the writer may manipulate conventions in a controlled way—especially grammar and spelling—for stylistic effect. √ Punctuation is accurate; it enables the reader to move through the text with understanding and ease. √ The writer's understanding of capitalization rules is evident throughout the paper. √ Most words, even difficult ones, are spelled correctly. √ The writing is long and complex enough to show the writer using a wide range of convention skills successfully.
Score 3	**Close. I Found a Few Errors.**
The writer of a Score 3 paper exhibits an awareness of a limited set of standard writing conventions and uses them to enhance the paper's readability. Some errors distract and confuse readers. Moderate editing is required before publication.	√ Paragraphs are used but may begin in the wrong places, or sections that should be separate paragraphs are run together. √ Conventions may not always be correct; however, problems with grammar and usage are usually not serious enough to distort meaning. √ End marks are usually correct, but other punctuation marks, such as commas, apostrophes, semicolons, and parentheses, may be missing or wrong. √ Common words are usually spelled correctly. √ Most words are capitalized correctly, but the writer's command of capitalization skills is inconsistent.
Score 1	**Hmm. I'm Distracted by Too Many Errors.**
In a Score 1 paper, there are errors in spelling, punctuation, grammar and usage, and paragraphing that seriously impede the reader's comprehension. Extensive editing is required for publication.	√ Paragraphing is missing, uneven, or too frequent. Most of the paragraphs do not reinforce or support the organizational structure of the paper. √ Errors in grammar and usage are very common and distracting; such errors also affect the paper's meaning. √ Punctuation, including end punctuation, is often missing or incorrect. √ Even common words are frequently misspelled. √ Capitalization is haphazard or reveals the writer's understanding of only the simplest rules. √ The paper must be read once just to decode the language and then again to capture the paper's meaning.

STUDENT/SELF-EVALUATION

Student/Self-Evaluation Rubrics for the Six Traits

Use these rubrics to evaluate your own writing. If you have a strong paper, you will be able to answer "yes" to the questions in the first box. Be honest! If your answers are "no," then go on to the next box. The questions in the second and third boxes will help you identify where your paper needs more work.

SIX TRAITS RUBRIC: IDEAS AND CONTENT

5 It's Crystal Clear!
√ Is my topic clearly focused—neither too broad nor too narrow—for a paper of this kind?
√ Are my ideas original, interesting, and creative?
√ Do I draw from personal experience or knowledge?
√ Are my details insightful and well chosen? Or are they obvious, predictable, or clichéd—not good?
√ Is my development of the topic thorough and logical? Have I anticipated and answered the reader's questions?
√ Are my supporting details accurate and relevant? Does my every detail contribute to the whole?

3 Close—It's Getting There.
√ Could I develop my topic a little better? Do I make my readers work to figure out my purpose and predict how ideas will develop?
√ Are my supporting details present but maybe too vague? Could they really illustrate the main idea or theme better?
√ Do I refer to my own experience or knowledge but maybe fail to push beyond the obvious to more specific ideas?
√ Are my ideas understandable but maybe not detailed, elaborated upon, or personalized? Do I need to work on understanding my topic or task more?
√ Do I stray from the topic? Are my ideas too general? Do I force readers to rely on what they already know to make sense of the paper?

1 Hmm. What Am I Trying to Say?
√ Have I forgotten to decide on a topic or main idea? Does my paper read like a rough draft or brainstorming notes?
√ Is my thesis a vague statement about the topic or a restatement of a prompt? Does it need more support, detail, or insight?
√ Do I need to add information? Do I make my readers work too hard to make connections?
√ Is my text rambling and repetitious? Are my ideas not developed enough? Is the paper too short?
√ Does every idea and detail in my paper seem equally weighted? Do my ideas fail to add up to a main idea, thesis, or theme?

STUDENT/SELF-EVALUATION

SIX TRAITS RUBRIC: ORGANIZATION

5 Yes! I Can See Where This Is Going.

√ Does my paper use a logical and effective sequence of ideas?

√ Does the paper contain both an attention-grabbing introduction and a satisfying conclusion?

√ Is my pacing carefully controlled? Do I slow down to provide explanation or elaboration when appropriate and increase the pace when necessary?

√ Do my transitions make clear connections and cue the reader to specific relationships between ideas?

√ Is my organizational structure appropriate to my purpose and audience?

√ If present, does my title sum up the central idea of the paper in a fresh way?

3 Close—Wait, I Think I Get It.

√ Does my paper have both an introduction and a conclusion? Are they as engaging and coherent as they can be?

√ Is my sequence logical but predictable? Could it be more compelling?

√ Does my sequence fail to consistently support my paper's ideas? Do I make my readers reorder sections mentally or provide transitions as they read?

√ Is my pacing reasonably well done? Do I move ahead too quickly or linger over unimportant ideas?

√ Are the transitions between ideas clear enough?

√ If present, is my title maybe a little dull or lacking insight?

1 Hmm. I'm a Little Lost.

√ Is the sequence in my paper broken—maybe one idea or event does not logically follow another? Does it lack organizational structure, such as clear paragraph breaks?

√ Does my paper lack a clear introduction to guide readers and a conclusion that sums up ideas at the end?

√ Is my pacing halting or inconsistent? Do I know when to slow down or speed up the pace in order to help my readers understand?

√ Are the transitions between my ideas confusing or absent?

√ If present, does my title accurately reflect the content of the paper? If not, why?

STUDENT/SELF-EVALUATION

SIX TRAITS RUBRIC: VOICE

5 Yes! I Can Really Hear My Own Voice.
√ Is the tone of my writing appropriate for the purpose and audience of the paper?
√ Do I reveal myself as a real person behind the text? Do I take risks in revealing my personality throughout the piece?
√ If my paper is expository or persuasive, do I show a strong connection to the topic and explain why readers should care about the issue?
√ If my paper is narrative, is my point of view sincere, interesting, and compelling?
3 Close. I Need To Try Again With Feeling.
√ Do I offer only generalities instead of personal insights? Does my writing feel impersonal?
√ Do I use neutral language and a flat tone instead of an interested, lively one?
√ Do I communicate in an earnest and pleasing manner, but forget to take risks? Do I need to inspire or engage my reader more?
√ Do I really share my own interest in the topic? Do I need to build more credibility with the audience?
√ Does my narrative fail to reveal a fresh or individual perspective?
1 Hmm. I Can Barely Hear Myself Speaking.
√ Is it true that I don't really think about the audience—that I use a voice that may not be appropriate for the intended reader?
√ Is the development of my topic too limited, so that no clear point of view is present? Is my writing so short that readers don't get to know me?
√ Do I seem to speak in a monotone, using a voice that lacks excitement about the message or topic?
√ Does my expository or persuasive writing lack accurate information or use overly technical language? Is my narrative writing lacking a point of view and failing to inspire interest?

STUDENT/SELF-EVALUATION

SIX TRAITS RUBRIC: WORD CHOICE

5 Yes! My Words Come Through Loud and Clear.

√ Are all my words specific and appropriate? In all instances, have I taken care to choose the right words or phrases?

√ Is my paper's language controlled and natural, not overdone? Have I mostly avoided using clichés and jargon?

√ Does my paper contain energetic verbs, precise nouns, and clear modifiers?

√ Do I use vivid words and phrases, including sensory details to create distinct images in the reader's mind?

3 Close—With a Little Polish My Words Will Shine.

√ Are my words correct and generally adequate but maybe lacking in originality or precision?

√ Do I use familiar words and phrases that do not grab the reader's interest or imagination or only occasionally use lively verbs and phrases to perk things up?

√ Do my attempts at using engaging or academic language seem overly showy?

√ Does my writing contain passive voice verbs and basic nouns and adjectives? Does it lack precise adverbs?

1 Hmm. Even I Don't Understand What I Mean.

√ Is my language perhaps too vague instead of precise? Does my vague language make the reader feel confused and unsure of my purpose?

√ Are some of my words or parts of speech used incorrectly?

√ Do I repeat myself or use certain words too much?

√ Have I used unexplained jargon or clichés?

STUDENT/SELF-EVALUATION

SIX TRAITS RUBRIC: SENTENCE FLUENCY

5 Yes! My Sentences Really Flow.

√ Have I constructed sentences so that meaning is clear to the reader?

√ Do my sentences vary in length and in structure?

√ Do I use varied sentence beginnings to add interest and clarity?

√ Does my writing have a steady rhythm? Is my reader able to read the text effortlessly without confusion or stumbling?

√ Is my use of dialogue natural? Do I use sentence fragments thoughtfully?

√ Do I use clear connectives and transitions between sentences to reveal how the paper's ideas work together?

3 Close—But I Feel As Though I'm Drifting Off Course.

√ Are my sentences usually grammatical and unified but dull? Have I forgotten to pay enough attention to how the sentences sound?

√ Is there some variation in sentence length and structure as well as in sentence beginnings? Or are all my sentences constructed exactly the same way?

√ Do I make my reader search for transitional words and phrases that show how sentences relate to one another? Do I forget to use context clues?

√ Even though I have written expressively, are there passages with stilted or awkward sentences?

1 Hmm. I'm a Little Lost.

√ Do my sentences just not "hang together"? Have I used run-on, incomplete, monotonous, or awkward sentences?

√ Does my phrasing often sound too singsong? Is my paper kind of dull to read aloud?

√ Do most of the sentences begin the same way and follow the same pattern (e.g., subject-verb-object)?

√ Have I used too many connectives or too few—so that my writing sometimes sounds confused?

STUDENT/SELF-EVALUATION

SIX TRAITS RUBRIC: CONVENTIONS

5 It's Nearly Perfect!

√ Is my paragraphing regular? Does it enhance the organization of the paper?

√ Are my grammar and usage correct? Do they add clarity and style to the text?

√ Is my punctuation accurate, and does it enable the reader to move though the text with understanding and ease?

√ Is my understanding of capitalization rules evident throughout the paper?

√ Are most words, even difficult ones, spelled correctly?

√ Is my writing long and complex enough to show that I understand a wide range of convention skills?

3 Close. I Found a Few Errors.

√ Do I run together ideas that should be in separate paragraphs? Do I start paragraphs in the middle of an idea?

√ Does my writing have a few grammar and usage errors—but not enough to confuse my readers?

√ Are my end marks usually in the correct place, but maybe other punctuation marks (such as commas, apostrophes, semicolons, and parentheses) are missing or wrong?

√ Have I spelled common words correctly for the most part?

√ Are most words capitalized correctly, but my command of capitalization skills is a little shaky?

1 Hmm. I'm Distracted by Too Many Errors.

√ Am I missing formal paragraphs? Do my paragraphs "forget" to support my content or organization?

√ Have I made a lot of errors in grammar and usage? Are there enough errors to distract or confuse the reader?

√ Is my punctuation, including end marks, often missing or incorrect?

√ Have I misspelled common words?

√ Have I consistently made errors in capitalization?

√ Does my paper need to be read once just to decode the language and then again to understand my meaning?

STUDENT/SELF-EVALUATION
PUBLISHING

5 Yes! My Paper Is Clear and Pleasing to the Eye.

√ If my paper is handwritten, is my writing neat and easy to read? Is my spacing between words uniform?

√ If my paper is word-processed, have I used an appropriate font and font size?

√ Have I used enough white space (spacing, margins) so that my paper is easy to read?

√ If I have included a title, headings or subheadings, bullets, and page numbering, are they consistent and do they make the paper easy to read?

√ If I have used graphs, tables, maps, or other graphics in my writing, are they clear and placed logically in my paper?

3 Close—My Paper Is a Little Cluttered.

√ Is my handwriting readable but maybe a little sloppy or inconsistent?

√ Have I used too many fonts or a font size that is hard to read?

√ Have I got too much or too little white space—my margins are too wide or too small? Have I got too much or too little space between paragraphs?

√ Even though I use titles, headings or subheadings, bullets, and page numbering, are they inconsistently used or maybe they get in the way of the reading?

√ Have I placed graphs, tables, maps, or other graphics in the wrong places or too far from the text they help explain? Do they take up too much space, or are they too small to read?

1 Hmm. I'm Distracted by the Way the Page Looks.

√ Has poor handwriting made my paper too difficult to read?

√ Has my use of interesting or too many fonts and font sizes made my paper difficult to read?

√ Is my spacing too random or confusing for readers to see and read the text?

√ Does my paper need a title, headings or subheadings, bullets, or page numbers that would help readers get through the paper?

√ Do my visuals (graphs, tables, maps, or other graphics) mislead or confuse my readers? Are they appropriate or too technical? Should I leave them out or find new ones?

Evaluation Chart

You can fill in the chart below as you evaluate your own or another student's writing. First write the scores you give the paper for its execution of each of the six writing traits. (The highest score is 5; the lowest is 1.) Then write some comments that explain the scores you gave. Use specific examples from the text to support your evaluations.

Six Trait Scores	
Trait	**Score**
Ideas and Content	
Organization	
Voice	
Word Choice	
Sentence Fluency	
Conventions	
Overall Comments:	

Six Traits for Writing Success, Middle School

ANSWER KEY

On the next three pages you will find three completed evaluation forms for the practice essays that appear on pages 44–45, 51–52, and 58–59. Use the scores on these evaluations to gauge your own evaluating skills.

page 30 Evaluating Voice

Possible responses:

stressin' about—worrying about

yakking with—talking with

it's a drag—it causes problems

messes up—ruins

page 46

COMPLETED EVALUATION CHART FOR EXPOSITORY ESSAY (PP. 44–45)

Six Trait Scores	
Trait	**Score**
Ideas and Content: The writer has a solid and clear interpretation of the quotation in the writing prompt. He or she makes three clear connections between wars and earthquakes.	4
Organization: The organization is relatively clear. The writer discusses three ways in which wars and earthquakes are alike, but the paragraphs don't follow a consistent organizational pattern. In some paragraphs, the writer talks about both war and earthquakes. In other paragraphs, the writer focuses on one or the other.	3
Voice: The writer's concern about the impact of wars and earthquakes is clear. Readers can sense the writer's personal feelings.	4
Word Choice: The writer's word choices are adequate. They convey his or her feelings and ideas, but they do not sparkle much.	3
Sentence Fluency: The writer does have some sentence variety in terms of mixing sentence lengths and having sentences with varied beginnings. He or she also uses transitional words and phrases consistently.	4
Conventions: The writer has a firm and consistent grasp of writing conventions.	5
Overall Comments:	
Overall I thought the paper was written with conviction and shows a good grasp of the impact of wars and earthquakes. The writer clearly felt strongly about his or her ideas, but the organization could have used some work. The paper is adequate.	

COMPLETED EVALUATION CHART FOR PERSUASIVE ESSAY (PP. 51–52)

Six Trait Scores	
Trait	**Score**
Ideas and Content: The writer repeats the prompt questions in the introduction without adding any original ideas. The writer takes a stand against uniforms, presents opposing views, and makes concessions, but then he or she seems wishy washy in the conclusion. The writer provides some good reasons, but some details are random and unrelated.	3
Organization: The paper is somewhat organized, but the writer sometimes meanders off topic.	2
Voice: The writer uses informal language that doesn't really suit the topic.	2
Word Choice: The writer's choice of words is adequate but somewhat repetitive.	3
Sentence Fluency: The paper contains sentence fragments and poorly constructed sentences. Transitions are barely used to show connections between ideas and sentences.	2
Conventions: The paper has many errors in punctuation, spelling, and grammar and usage.	2
Overall Comments:	
Overall I thought the paper was probably written quickly and without much planning. The writer's argument is weakened by distracting details, informal language, and a weak conclusion. The writer clearly needs to brush up on the conventions of writing.	

COMPLETED EVALUATION CHART FOR NARRATIVE ESSAY (PP. 58–59)

Six Trait Scores	
Trait	**Score**
Ideas and Content: The writer tells an original story that conveys a lesson she has learned. The story is original and interesting and filled with details that appeal to the senses.	5
Organization: The narrative tells events in the order they occurred and uses pacing to build suspense.	5
Voice: The writer's voice is really apparent here. Through dialogue, inner monologue, and details, the writer reveals her original thoughts and feelings during the experience. The voice really engages the reader.	5
Word Choice: The writer chooses words carefully, and she successfully conveys the experience. Her language appeals to the senses, and her dialogue sounds realistic and fresh.	5
Sentence Fluency: The sentences are varied and well constructed and often sophisticated. They contain transitions that help readers follow the course of events in the story. The sentences flow so nicely that readers are not distracted. They can pay attention to the events of the story.	5
Conventions: The writer has a clear and consistent grasp of writing conventions.	5
Overall Comments:	
Overall I thought the paper was excellent. The writer obviously enjoyed writing it. Her writing is vivid and interesting, and her voice is lively. The writer clearly learned something from her uncle and wanted to share her experience with others. Well done!	

page 63 Reading and Analyzing Prompts

Prompt 1
Topic: something I am proud of
Purpose: to tell a story about a personal experience
Audience: general audience

Prompt 2
Topic: my stand on a 9pm curfew
Purpose: to defend my position
Audience: editor of newspaper, newspaper readers

Prompt 3
Topic: concept of honor
Purpose: to explain the meaning of honor
Audience: school newspaper readers

ANSWERS FOR WORKSHEETS ON VOICE, WORD CHOICE, SENTENCE FLUENCY, AND CONVENTIONS

page 101 Identifying Tone

Possible responses:

Passage 1: Possible tones: formal, whiny, slightly unreasonable

Reason: The writer sounds like he or she is complaining by focusing on the unfairness. He or she repeats the word "unfair" several times and uses qualifying phrases such as "one bit of credit," "really unfair," and "plain unfair."

Passage 2: Possible tones: informal, conversational, disrespectful

Reason: The tone sounds like someone speaking—like one teen speaking to another. The writer uses slang and disrespectful terms, such as "Duh!" and "Whatever."

Passage 3: Possible tones: reasonable, formal, thoughtful

Reason: The writer sounds as though he or she respects the audience and cares about the topic. He or she uses "we" as well as formal language.

page 102 Recognizing Connotations

Possible responses:

1. *naughty* **Definition:** not behaved; **Connotation:** When you are naughty, you are mischievous in a cute kind of way.

2. *challenging* **Definition:** difficult, hard; **Connotation:** Challenging means "difficult in a way that makes a person stretch or try to improve him or herself."

3. *oozed* **Definition:** flowed or leaked; **Connotation:** Here the word sounds like a leak that is disgusting or yucky.

4. *recognition* **Definition:** acknowledgement; **Connotation:** Recognition means "not only being seen but also being given approval."

5. *sensitive* **Definition:** easily affected; **Connotation:** The word suggests that the person is too easily affected and is actually kind of annoying.

page 103 Avoiding Loaded Language, Jargon, and Clichés

1. **C:** let the cat out of the bag

2. **LL:** honest, hardworking Americans

3. **J:** run the numbers

4. **C:** pretty as a picture

5. **C:** red as a lobster

6. **J:** Wall Street, the Dow and NASDAQ

7. **J:** log on, password, PIN

8. **LL:** quacks

9. **C:** hit the roof

10. **LL:** incompetent bureaucrat, waste

11. **J:** scan, bar code

12. **C:** flat as a pancake

13. **C or LL:** great, very unique

14. **LL:** fat cat politicians

15. **LL:** wannabes and posers

page 104 Avoiding Passive Voice

1. **PV:** Sharmaine served the tennis ball.

2. **AV:** no correction needed

3. **PV:** Several new people attended the class.

4. **PV:** Many tourists view the art in the museum.

5. **PV:** A tree trimmer pruned our pecan tree.

6. **PV:** The veterinarian gave the dog its rabies vaccination.

7. **PV:** The technician fixed the computer.

8. **AV:** no correction needed

9. **AV:** no correction needed

10. **PV:** A local nursery donated the plants for the school garden.

11. **AV:** no correction needed

12. **PV:** The postal worker delivered the package.

page 105 Revising Passive Voice

Below is the paragraph with the "to be" verbs underlined.

The arctic tundra is characterized by long winters, little snow, and low temperatures. Warm summer temperatures thaw the tundra's surface soil but not the subsoil, or permafrost. Therefore, drainage is hindered by flat and partially frozen ground. Ponds and bogs are formed by standing water. Typical arctic vegetation includes low plants, such as cotton grass, sedge, and lichens. Soil disturbances such as "flowing soil" are caused by thaws and movement of soil. Irregular landforms, such as hummocks, frost boils, and earth stripes, are produced by poorly drained areas. On the soft surface, deep gullies are caused by vehicle tracks. Most arctic vegetation can survive these soil disturbances. Likewise, arctic wildlife is also not deeply affected by these changes.

Corrected version. Possible revision.

Long winters, little snow, and low temperatures characterize the arctic tundra. Warm summer temperatures thaw the tundra's surface soil but not the subsoil, or permafrost. Therefore, flat and partially frozen ground hinders drainage. Standing water forms ponds and bogs. Typical arctic vegetation includes low plants, such as cotton grass, sedge, and lichens. Thaws and movement of soil cause soil disturbances such as "flowing soil." Poorly drained areas produce irregular landforms, such as hummocks, frost boils, and earth stripes. On the soft surface, vehicle tracks form deep gullies. Most arctic vegetation can survive these soil disturbances. These changes do not deeply affect arctic wildlife either.

page 106 Revising for Sentence Variety
Possible revision:

The Populist movement was an American movement that developed in the 1800s. It began during the depression of the late 1870s, when farmers were losing money. They formed organized groups called Farmers' Alliances. Members of the alliances worked together. They built barns for storing the crops, which stayed in the barns until the prices were better. Some alliances included African American farmers. Although African American farmers could not vote, the alliances welcomed them anyway.

The alliances became powerful at the end of the century and formed a national political party. They joined forces with another group called the Knights of Labor. The two groups formed the People's Party, and its members were known as Populists. Populists wanted the national government to change. They wanted it to print more paper money because more paper money might raise farm prices. The Populists also wanted a national income tax. Americans did not pay income tax then. Although it was not a popular idea, it became a reality when Congress passed the sixteenth amendment in 1913, which made a national income tax legal. Americans have paid income tax ever since.

page 107 Revising Run-on Sentences
The revised passage should appear as follows:

Today when modern meteorologists forecast the weather, they can count on the help of an impressive battery of scientific devices. Weather satellites, for example, relay photographs of cloud formations from all over the world. These pictures show where storms are beginning over oceans and deserts. The paths of typhoons and hurricanes are tracked the same way. Weather information from all sources is fed into powerful computers. Thus the weather can be evaluated with amazing speed.

Our ancestors had no complicated weather instruments. They had to rely on their eyes and ears and a few old proverbs and maxims. Their methods were hardly scientific. Today, for example, no one still believes the old superstition about the groundhog, but we celebrate Groundhog Day just the same. The story goes that if the groundhog sees its shadow on the second day of February, there will be six more weeks of winter. Watch for yourself and see! The behavior of insects, on the other hand, is still a good indicator of temperature because they are cold blooded. Grasshoppers cannot fly when the temperature drops below 55 degrees Fahrenheit. If you hear a cricket chirping, count the number of chirps in fourteen seconds and add forty. Then you will have the temperature in degrees Fahrenheit.

Today weather forecasting is much more accurate if less charming than it was in the old days.

However, the forecasters are still not always right, perhaps because there are so many factors to consider.

page 108 Revising Stringy Sentences

Possible revision:

Argentina is a country in South America. It borders the south Atlantic, and its capital is Buenos Aires. My friend Leela has been to Argentina. She went with her family while her father studied at a university there. Leela had a great time meeting people, and she got to speak in Spanish. Leela spent time in the city, but she also went to the countryside, where she learned about the life of the cowboys of South America. She was very impressed, so she wrote a story about her experiences. It is about a character named Tanmoor. He is an interesting character even though he is from a small town in Argentina. However, he wants to move to the big city. The story has an interesting beginning. It opens with Tanmoor's father working on a ranch. He is a vaquero—a cowboy—and the bank wants to put him out of business. Tanmoor is trying to help save the ranch. Leela clearly did lots of research and asked a lot of questions. It shows because the story is excellent!

page 109 Revising Wordy Sentences

Possible revision:

When the daughters of pioneers were young girls, they learned how to sew and cook. Young girls had to learn household skills because otherwise the chores wouldn't get done. So girls would carefully and thoughtfully attend their mother's instructions. They had to do all sorts of chores that we don't even do anymore, like make butter, bake bread, and wash clothes by hand. Today we have convenient machines to do household chores. In addition, we never have to cook because we can go to the grocery store and buy any ready-to-eat food we want. Life was hard for pioneer women, and we should be grateful that we can get many jobs done with the flip of a switch.

page 110 Choppy Sentences and Sentence Combining

Possible revisions:

1. The Himalayas are the tallest mountains in Asia.

2. Tea bushes grow on steep slopes on the fertile hills near Darjeeling.

3. The great danger in climbing comes from the high altitude and the bitter cold.

4. Marissa's family will hike in Rocky Mountain National Park and pitch tents in Hidden Valley.

5. Mrs. Goldstein jogs in the park every morning and walks her dog every evening.

6. Bruce received a beautiful wall hanging from his grandmother in Vietnam.

7. Helga bought new running shoes during the sale.

page 111 Using Transitional Words and Phrases

The transitional words and phrases are underlined.

After dinner, we sang songs around the campfire and told stories. As the cool night air arrived,

I pulled out my sleeping bag and unrolled it. Then Jeb and I took the pails down to the stream and filled them. We set them beside the fire and waited. Meanwhile everyone seemed to be dozing off. When I was certain that everyone was asleep, I used the water in the bucket to douse the fire. The hot logs sizzled as a result of being splashed with cold water.

Then I climbed into my sleeping bag and looked at the stars above me. Although I had spent a lot of time in the country, I had trouble remembering the formal names of the constellations. My father had tried to teach me, but I forgot. So I invented my own names, and I remembered them, too. Eventually I fell asleep and dreamed I could float in the sky like the stars.

The next morning, the first thing I did was restart the fire. I knew the campers would never forgive me if they had to wait for their breakfasts. More important, I did not want to wait long for my first cup of coffee. Otherwise I would be very grumpy.

page 112 Paragraphing

The first paragraph should end after "fun things to do." The second paragraph should begin "Those who don't agree" and end with "I could go to after school." The third paragraph should begin with "Finally, I believe."

The paragraph breaks occur when the writer identifies and explains a new point.

page 113 Usage: Verb Agreement

1. My sisters never (*enjoy, enjoys*) ice skating anymore.

2. The club members (*is, are*) planning an overnight hike.

3. No one but Jacqueline (*want, wants*) to go.

4. The local newspaper (*doesn't, don't*) print much foreign news.

5. Anybody who is interested in boats (*need, needs*) to know how to swim.

6. Neither of my grandmothers (*has, have*) retired.

7. Few of the documents (*was, were*) authentic.

8. Not one of the astronomers (*know, knows*) whether life exists on Mars.

9. Among writers, some (*has, have*) made predictions that came true.

10. A fleet of ships (*are, is*) sailing into the harbor.

11. Deneice and Maria (*play, plays*) volleyball after school.

12. Neither Ellie nor Noah (*read, reads*) much science fiction.

13. Ms. Galinsky or Mr. Wilson (*have, has*) the details about the meeting.

14. (*Has, Have*) the committee checked the date for its next meeting?

15. (*Don't, Doesn't*) the falling rain sound beautiful?

16. The dogs (*wag, wags*) their tails with excitement.

17. Flocks of birds (_fly_, flies) over our house on their way south for winter.

18. Bottles of water (was, _were_) waiting for the runners at the finish line.

19. Some of the puzzle pieces (is, _are_) straight on one edge.

20. Which sandwiches (has, _have_) only peanut butter on them?

21. During the summer, all of the beaches (is, _are_) crowded with tourists.

22. Frank and Sarah's new car (run, _runs_) on electricity.

23. The flags around the ballpark (wave, _waves_) in the breeze.

24. The scent of the roses in the field (fill, _fills_) the air.

25. The rocks (gain, _gains_) speed as they roll down the hillside.

page 114 Usage: Verb Tense

The following revised paragraph uses verbs in the past tense:

Eleanor Roosevelt's parents died when she was a child, so she was raised by her grandmother and sent to school in England. There she fell under the influence of headmistress Marie Souvestre, who worked for social causes. As a young adult, Roosevelt participated in social work before she married Franklin Delano Roosevelt. After her husband entered politics, she worked for the American Red Cross during World War I and later became more involved in politics herself. In the early 1930s, Mrs. Roosevelt became a leading activist for women's rights. When her husband was elected President of the United States, Mrs. Roosevelt helped other women get appointed to government positions. She traveled around the country, visited coal mines and slums, and spoke out for the poor. After her husband's death, Mrs. Roosevelt was appointed by President Truman to be a delegate to the United Nations. Her service to the U.N. was probably her greatest achievement. Eleanor Roosevelt devoted her whole life to causes of humanity and was loved by many.

page 115 Standard Usage

1. have

2. bad

3. effects

4. less

5. those

6. choose

7. that

8. try to

9. themselves

10. very

11. isn't

12. except

13. why

14. broke

15. among

16. good

17. A

18. that

19. as if

20. than

21. Advertisers

22. is

23. teach

24. outside

25. somewhat

page 116 Capitalization and Spelling

Corrected passage (corrected words are underlined):

America's food has been influenced by many cultures. Who has not enjoyed Chinese egg drop soup, Italian pasta, Mexican tacos, or the German and Scandinavian cheeses from Wisconsin. The smorgasbord may seem American, but the idea originated in Sweden. Pretzels were originally Dutch delicacies. Shish kebab, which is often served at backyard barbecues, is actually a Turkish dish. No Thanksgiving dinner would be complete without turkey, corn, and pumpkin. These foods are truly American, for they were here long before the pilgrims reached North America.

Corrected passage (corrected words are underlined):

The Regional Art Club includes members from middle schools in twenty-two cities. Art critics throughout the state concede that our members are extremely talented. "Use your imagination" and "Express your creativity" are our mottos. We have large studios at four centrally located schools. There is a large variety of artistic styles among our members. Some students make huge sculptures out of metal objects. The club is overrun with painters, as you might expect. Potters easily come in second in number. Photography is also a popular art, especially with many students in the ninth grade. Members usually meet once during the week and again on Saturdays.

page 117 Punctuation

Corrected passage (corrections are underlined):

One hundred years ago, there were a hundred thousand elephants living in Asia; however, now there are only about one third of that number. What an alarming loss! The Asian elephant is now an endangered species for the following reasons: cutting of forests, other damage to habitat, and increased human population. Of the Asian elephants that remain, about ten thousand live in the small country of Myanmar. Can you find the country in the atlas? It is located between Thailand and Bangladesh. Many of the huge, patient elephants, also called timber elephants, work with humans; together they bring in large, valuable trees to sell for lumber. The elephants and the people have a partnership, and they spend their lives together. This partnership is remarkable for the mutual affection and trust it demonstrates between animals and humans.

Corrected passage (corrections are underlined):

"I propose that the group take a canoe trip down the Delaware!" said Nicky with enthusiasm. "We could rent canoes in Callicoon and paddle down to Bingham Falls."

"I think that is a good idea," Charlotte replied, "but how do we get the canoes back to Callicoon?"

"That's easy," Nicky answered, "because there is a series of posts along the river where we can leave the canoes. We rent them at one post and check them at a post farther down the river."

"Let's schedule the trip for next weekend!" Bryce exclaimed.